Hiker's Guide
to the
Mountains
of
New Hampshire

Hiker's Guide
to the
Mountains
of
New Hampshire

by
Jared Gange

Huntington Graphics
Burlington, Vermont

Graphic design, map implementation and typesetting
John A. Hadden, Resting Lion Studio, Huntington, Vermont

Editing
Linda Young and Elisabeth Podesta

ISBN 1-886064-18-0
Printed in Canada
Second Edition

Disclaimer:
Hiking, like many outdoor endeavors, is a potentially dangerous activity. Participants in these activities assume responsibility for their actions and safety. No guide book can replace good judgment on the part of the user. Obtain the necessary skills and inform yourself about potential dangers before taking part in outdoor recreation activities. Neither the author nor publisher, nor anyone associated with this book, has any responsibility or liability for anyone who uses the information contained herein or who participates in the sport of hiking. Hike difficulty ratings, time estimates, or impressions are subjective and will vary from hiker to hiker depending on such things as ability, experience, confidence, or physical fitness. As a result, the author cannot assure the accuracy of the information in this book, including hike descriptions, maps, and directions. These may be unintentionally misleading or incorrect.

Also note that access to hiking areas may be changed or revoked at any time. Hikers must be aware that publication of this book does not grant them permission nor a right to use the land on which the hikes mentioned in this book are located. Please obey posted signs that indicate a change in ownership or status of a trail or activity area.

Cover photo: Mts. Washington and Eisenhower from Mt. Pierce, Jared Gange
Photo opposite page: West Bond from Bondcliff, Robert Kozlow
Photo page 14: Robert Bailey
Photo page 16-17: Aerial view, east side of Mt. Washington (Mt. Washington Observatory)

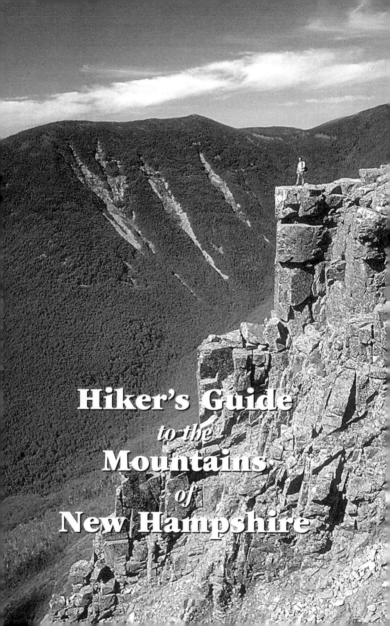

Hiker's Guide
to the
Mountains
of
New Hampshire

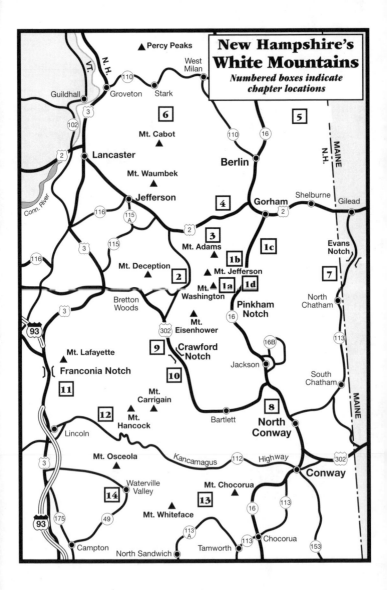

New Hampshire's White Mountains
Numbered boxes indicate chapter locations

▲ Percy Peaks

N.H.

VT.

(110)

West Milan

Guildhall

Groveton   Stark

(3)

(102)

6

Mt. Cabot ▲

(110)   (16)

5

(2)

Lancaster

Mt. Waumbek ▲

Berlin

Conn. River

Jefferson

Shelburne

(116)

(115 A)

(115)

4

Gorham

(2)

Gilead

MAINE   N.H.

(3)

3

Mt. Adams ▲

1c

Evans Notch

(116)

Mt. Deception ▲

2

1b

▲ Mt. Jefferson

1a

Mt. Washington ▲

1d

7

North Chatham

Bretton Woods

Pinkham Notch

(16)

(3)

Mt. Eisenhower ▲

(302)

9   **Crawford Notch**

(16B)

(113)

Mt. Lafayette ▲

10

Jackson

South Chatham

Franconia Notch

11

Mt. Carrigain ▲

Bartlett

8

North Conway

MAINE

12

Mt. Hancock ▲

Lincoln

Kancamagus   (112)   Highway

(302)   **Conway**

Mt. Osceola ▲

(3)

Waterville Valley

Mt. Chocorua ▲

13

(16)

(113)

14

(49)

Mt. Whiteface ▲

(93)

(175)

(113 A)

North Sandwich   Tamworth   (113)   Chocorua

(153)

(93)

Contents

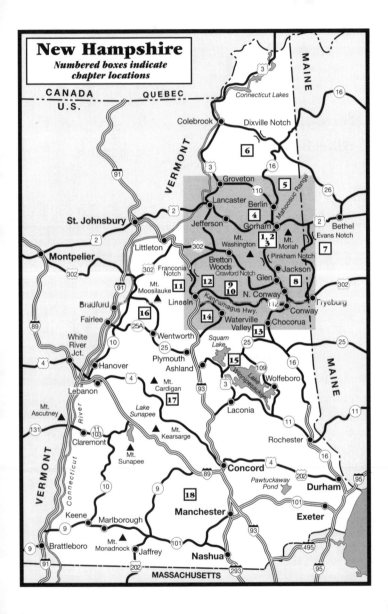

On the Bondcliff Trail   Robert Kozlow

The Forest Service has instituted a parking pass for the WMNF. Most trailhead parking areas require payment of a fee: $3 for one day, $5 for a week, and $20 for a year. Passes can be obtained at the trailheads, Forest Service district offices and many stores in the region. Parking passes must be displayed in your car when parked at a designated fee parking site.

In this guide, we emphasize hikes which can be accomplished in a day—sometimes a long day—but we include some popular overnight trips. We have given lengthier descriptions for about 30 hikes—trips that in our opinion every hiker will want to do. They are listed in the *Classic Hikes* appendix for quick reference. For those wanting to climb all of New Hampshire's mountains over 4,000', we provide at least one route on each of the 48 official summits. The Appalachian Mountain Club's 4,000'-er Committee can assist hikers — "peakbaggers" — in these pursuits.

In any event, we can only agree with Thomas Starr King in his classic guide to the area, *The White Hills, Their Legends, Landscape and Poetry* (published in 1859): "There is ample reward, as we shall hope to show, in any method of approach. Whichever path travellers may select, they cannot err in this delicious region."

Rating Hikes for Difficulty

The best measure of a hike's difficulty or, rather, the overall effort required to complete the hike, is the actual walking time needed. Since individual hiking speeds vary so much, the obvious question is, "The amount of time for whom?" The rating method we prefer considers the time for a more or less average hiker, hiking at a steady pace. The point is to provide a measure—an index—that works for most hikers most of the time. Thus, by comparing your actual times with the given times, you should soon be able to reliably predict how long you will need for a given hike. The times in the guide book are determined by a standard formula based on distance and elevation gain, and adjusted for the actual trail. Strong hikers in excellent shape will be able to reduce these times by a third or even half; others, in less of a hurry, will take longer

The method of an "idealized" hiking time as a measure of effort, although common in Europe, is not universally accepted in this country. But time is the only composite measure we have, and in mountainous terrain, distance alone as a measure of effort is very misleading. Time takes into account the objective factors of amount of climbing, steepness, trail quality, and difficulty in following the route, as well as distance. And only time can easily and accurately be measured by the hiker on the trail. However, so-called "subjective" conditions, such as wet or icy rocks, muddy trails, blowdowns, difficult stream crossings, wind, fog, or snow can greatly increase the time needed to complete a route. Thus we emphasize that the number of hours given is not offered as an actual time. Rather, it is offered as a standardized estimate. The time must be modified according to prevailing conditions.

Trails can be difficult in various ways: Some are relentlessly steep for hundreds or thousands of feet (Flume Slide); others are tough because the footing or passage is awkward (King Ravine); and still others involve "scrambling" up steep rock (Huntington Ravine). Finally, some trails have an element of danger: loose rocks, the possibility of a fall, remoteness from help in case of injury, or distance to shelter in a storm.

Mountain Weather

Aside from overestimating one's physical condition, the main cause of accidents and distress for hikers is weather. High on a mountain, miles from shelter, a perfect, sunny day quickly turns overcast, the wind picks up, and rain or snow pelts down. Will you be able to stay warm and dry? Should you continue or turn back? Is there a shorter way to safety? Do you, and everyone in your party, have the reserves of food and stamina to stay out longer than originally planned and under more adverse conditions? Will you be able to find your way in reduced visibility? The scenario posed above can easily become a reality; for most hikers it will sooner or later. Be prepared!

One seemingly obvious word of advice which is frequently ignored: When the weather is bad *before* starting out—the mountain tops are obscured in clouds, and it's raining or snowing—put it off for another day! No matter how long you may have planned the trip or how far you have driven, if the weather is bad, don't risk it. The mountains will always be there.

Exercising Good Judgment

Over many years, thousands of people at all times of the year have used the trails described in this guide. We have made an effort to present you with the best mountain hikes in the state: to point them out, to explain how to find them, and to give a brief description of each trip, including hiking time, round trip distance, and amount of climbing. The rest is up to you!

Hiking, like most outdoor activities, has some elements of danger. This is especially true above treeline or in stormy conditions, as briefly discussed above. It is your responsibility to understand these dangers, to make necessary preparations, and to take the appropriate precautions. This book is not—nor is any other guide book—a substitute for sound judgment on your part.

Maps

The United States Geological Survey (USGS) provides topographic maps for New Hampshire and the entire United States. Three map formats are currently in use. The most widely used is the 7.5-minute series at the 1:24 000 scale. In a few areas, these maps have been replaced by a 1:25 000 metric format, with twice the area—often referred to as "7.5 x 15 minute." Both formats display information at a detailed level, and show most hiking trails. However, many of the 7.5-minute quadrangles were drawn over 20 years ago and do not provide up-to-date trail information.

The USGS also provides a 1:100 000 scale metric series (1 degree by 30 minutes.) Although these maps lack the detail of the two series mentioned above, they are useful in gaining an understanding of a larger area, such as a county. The maps show major hiking trails, and the contour interval is 20 meters. Both metric map styles come folded, with a cover, as opposed to the loose sheet style of the non-metric series.

There are a number of hiking maps produced by the AMC, other hiking clubs, and various mapping companies. *Mount Washington and the Heart of the Presidential Range,* surveyed by Bradford Washburn, is the best map available for the Mount Washington area. The State of New Hampshire produces topographic map hand-out sheets for a number of areas, including Mount Monadnock, Franconia Notch, and Mount Sunapee. In addition to its useful Atlas and Gazetteer, DeLorme Mapping Company produces a comprehensive map of the White Mountains; Map Adventures produces the excellent *White Mountains Trail Map* and *White Mountains Hiking*; Topaz Maps offers a superb recreation map for the entire state of NH—*New Hampshire Outdoor Map*; and Wilderness Map Co. publishes a series of excellent topo maps: *Crawford Notch, Franconia Notch, Kancamagus Highway, Mount Washington, and White Mountains Hiking Guide (7 maps)*; and the Wonalancet Out Door Club's *Trail Map and Guide to the Sandwich Range Wilderness*, is also excellent. These maps and others are referred to throughout the book, usually at the end of the chapters—please look in the *References* section for complete information on maps and map sources.

Maps in this guide

The maps provided in this guide are intended as an aid to finding the trailheads and showing the general route of the various trails and their intersections. They will also give you some idea of the topography. The map shown below explains our use of symbols and serves as the legend for the maps throughout the book.

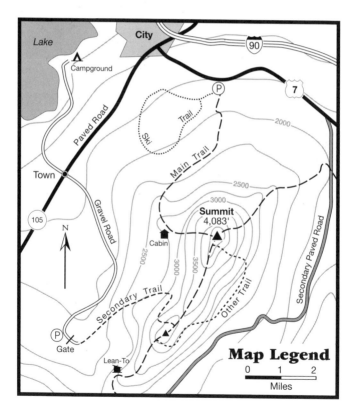

Lake

City

90

Campground

P

7

Ski Trail

2000

Paved Road

Main Trail

2500

Town

105

3000

Summit
4,083'

N

Cabin

2500

3000

3500

Secondary Paved Road

Secondary Trail

Other Trail

P

Gate

Lean-To

Map Legend

0   1   2

Miles

Camping

Throughout the book, we note Forest Service and state park campgrounds, as well as mountain huts and shelters. There are many private campgrounds in New Hampshire, especially in the White Mountains. For example, in the North Conway area (Mt. Washington), excellent campgrounds dot the Saco River's shores. The State of New Hampshire publishes a free state map showing campgrounds. Backcountry camping—camping away from trails—is permitted in the WMNF. See page 99 for more information on low-impact hiking and camping.

Hiking with Children

Most of the shorter hikes in this book, and the beginning sections of the longer hikes, are suitable for children. Views, especially distant views, do not always hold much fascination for kids. Their interests are usually closer at hand: stream crossings, bridges, rocky scrambles, a lake, or a hut. Take plenty of favorite snacks, walk at their pace, and set reasonable goals. Bringing a same-aged friend along is often a great motivator. Start out with very short trips, and if the interest is there, go with it! Hikes that last three or four hours, even with a moderate amount of climbing, are well within the reach of motivated 6- or 7-year-olds. See page 213 for a quick reference guide, *Hiking with Children*, which refers to suitable hikes in the book.

Hiking Tips

- Allow yourself plenty of time.

- Be realistic about your physical condition. If you are new to hiking, or have not hiked for some time, you will tend to underestimate the amount of time you will need.

- Start out with easy trips. Build confidence and experience gradually.

- Be prepared for worsening weather. Summits are usually cooler and breezier than lower elevations, and what starts out as a beautiful day can dissolve into harsh conditions.

- Consider the size of your group when planning your trip. The larger the group, the more time you will need.

- Let someone know your plans, or leave a note giving your planned route and estimated return time.

- Do not leave valuable items in your car, as break-ins do occasionally occur. (As a corollary to this and the previous tip, don't leave your trip plan in plain view in your car.)

- Be very careful about planning to descend by a difficult route you are unfamiliar with, especially on longer trips. Route finding problems, steep sections, stream crossings, etc. will put a tired and possibly overtaxed party at further risk.

- Pets should be controlled at all times. Some trails—those with ladders, for example—are often too difficult for dogs.

- Take drinking water with you. Even the clearest mountain stream may contain the Giardia parasite.

- Pack out what you pack in.

- Be especially careful when hiking alone.

- Try to have the lowest impact possible on the backcountry.

Mount Washington (6,288')

1A	**Mt. Washington's East Side**

Located at the base of the fabled Tuckerman Ravine Trail and on the Appalachian Trail, Pinkham Notch is a mecca for hikers and spring skiers. From here, many thousands make the spectacular and strenuous 4-mile hike up Mount Washington every year. With a vertical gain of 4,270', some very steep sections, and its upper third above treeline, this is a very serious hike by New England standards. The AMC's Pinkham Notch Visitor Center is one of the finest facilities for hikers in the United States. Pinkham Notch is located on the east side of Mt. Washington, 10 miles north of Jackson and 11 miles south of Gorham on NH 16. The photograph shows Mt. Washington in the spring: Tuckerman Ravine is on the left, and Huntington Ravine is on the right.

and Pinkham Notch

Tuckerman Ravine Trail

From **Pinkham Notch Visitor Center** the wide, pleasant trail parallels Cutler River, passing **Crystal Cascade** after about 15 minutes and **Boott Spur Trail** (on the left) soon after. Maintaining its width (it is actually a rough tractor road) the trail is much rockier once it starts to climb. **Huntington Ravine Trail** departs right at 1.3 miles and **Raymond Path** at 2.1 miles. After about 1½–2 hours and 2.4 miles, the shelters and caretaker's cabin at **Hermit Lake** come into view; this is affectionately known as **HoJo's**. Here, at the base of the ravine, the impressive flank of **Boott Spur** (with skiers' **Hillman Highway**) looms overhead. Above, on the right, are the ramparts of **Lion Head**, Tuckerman Ravine's north wall. Although you are now over halfway to the top in terms of distance, the remaining portion usually takes at least as long as the lower part. After a brief wooded section, the trail is in the open and climbs steeply at times, reaching the innermost recesses of the ravine about 30 minutes from Hermit Lake. In a sense, this is the best part of the trip. Yes, panoramic views of "forest and crag" await at the summit, but it is here, working your way up the **headwall** of this high alpine basin—a classic glacial cirque—that many hikers get their first taste of an alpine environment. Clamber out of the ravine: The grade eases, and the path soon passes the **Alpine Garden Trail** before coming to **Tuckerman Junction**. Bear right here and follow the route up the final slopes—the summit cone—over and across large boulders. The summit may come as a shock: buildings, lots of people, cars, the cog railway, and the main building with its cafeteria, museum exhibits, souvenirs, etc. The observation platform gives a less cluttered view. Return by the same route.

8–9 hours, 8.2 miles, total climb: 4,270'

Approach: *Park at the AMC's Pinkham Notch Visitor Center on NH 16.*

Note: *Snow and ice on the trail may keep Tuckerman Ravine closed to hikers until early June. Check with the Forest Service or the AMC.*

Mount Washington via Lion Head

The **Lion Head Trail** branches right from the Tuckerman Ravine Trail 2.3 miles from Pinkham Notch, at a point just below the first of the Hermit Lake shelters and where Boott Spur Link departs left. Lion Head Trail is the most important variation of the Tuckerman Ravine Trail, and a variation of it is the winter route up Mt. Washington. From Tuckerman Ravine Trail, the Lion Head Trail climbs steeply for a half mile before coming into the open. The views into Tuckerman Ravine from the ridge are dramatic. With its upper section on much easier ground, Lion Head Trail crosses Alpine Garden Trail on grassy slopes and climbs to meet **Tuckerman Ravine Trail** 0.4 mile below the summit. Descend the way you came or, for variety, via Tuckerman Ravine or Bigelow Lawn and Boott Spur (see below).

8 hours, 8.6 miles, elevation gain: 4,270'

Approach: *Start from the Pinkham Notch Visitor Center.*

Boott Spur

The **Boott Spur Trail** branches left off the **Tuckerman Ravine Trail** 0.4 mile above Pinkham, or about 15 minutes out. It winds through dense woods, passing several side trails (to views), finally breaking into the open just before **Split Rock**, about 2.5 miles from Pinkham. Continue along the ridge of Boott Spur with terrific views into the Ravine and directly over to Lion Head. At **Davis Path**, stay right, and after 0.6 mile bear right on **Lawn Cutoff** to **Tuckerman Junction**, taking the Tuckerman Ravine Trail to the top. Return via Tuckerman Ravine Trail (or Boott Spur). Note that the Boott Spur route is more exposed to the elements (above treeline longer) than Tuckerman Ravine, so extra caution is advised.

Round trip: 9 hours, 9.5 miles, elevation gain: 4,270'

Variation: Descending Boott Spur provides an interesting (and somewhat longer) variation on the usual Tuckerman Ravine Trail: From **Tuckerman Junction**, head south on **Lawn Cutoff** to **Davis Path**. Here bear left, reaching **Boott Spur Trail** after about 15 minutes. Continue on this down to Pinkham Notch.

The Alpine Garden

In June this really is a garden—a showcase of alpine flowers. A gently sloping shelf between the steeper summit cone above and the cliffs of Huntington Ravine below, the Alpine Garden is reached most easily by driving up the Auto Road to the parking area just before the 7-mile mark, at the top of the **Huntington Ravine Trail**. Hike down the trail a short way before branching right on the **Alpine Garden Trail** and easier terrain. Return the same way. To hike up, take **Lion Head Trail** (see above), reaching the Alpine Garden Trail at 3.4 miles. Here, walk left or right along the trail as you please, returning to Pinkham Notch by Lion Head. When approaching from **Lakes of the Clouds**, take **Tuckerman Crossover** and continue through **Tuckerman Junction** on the Tuckerman Ravine Trail to the Alpine Garden Trail on the left.

Approach: From the Auto Road, Pinkham Notch, or Lakes of the Clouds.

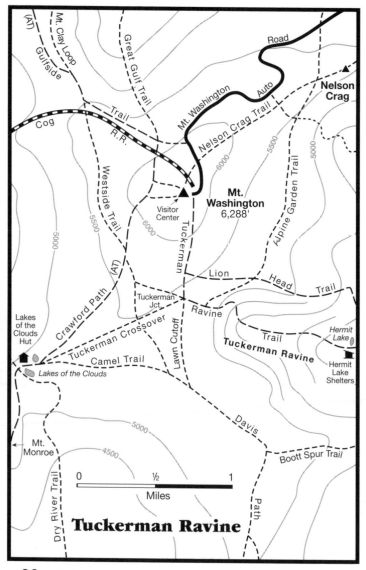

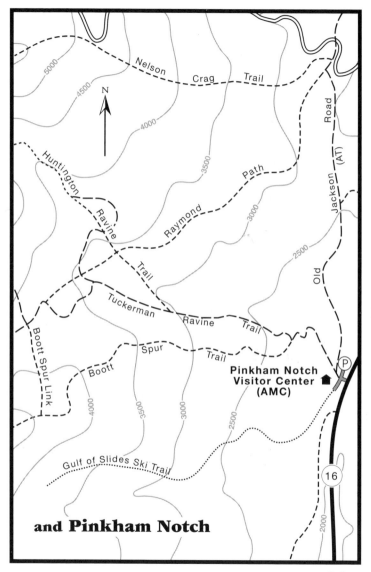

and **Pinkham Notch**

Glen Boulder   Robert Kozlow

Huntington Ravine

As Tuckerman Ravine draws hikers and skiers, Huntington Ravine beckons ice climbers. But while the ice climber has many classic routes to choose from, Huntington Ravine offers the hiker only *one* route, and a very difficult one! In fact, the headwall portion of this route is more of a rock climb (a "scramble") than a trail—it is the hardest hiking route in the White Mountains. Its degree of difficulty is an order of magnitude greater than anything else in this book. Climb it only in dry conditions; it is not usually descended. Follow **Tuckerman Ravine Trail** for 1.3 miles, then branch right on narrow, wooded **Huntington Ravine Trail**. After negotiating several possibly difficult streams (high water, slippery rocks), cross **Raymond Path** 1.8 miles from Pinkham and a fire road soon after. Then, after a steep section, the trail reaches the boulder-strewn floor of the ravine. The yellow-blazed route now ascends the lower slabs and works its way up a series of cliffs. Use cracks and crevices for hand and footholds; exercise great care. Some sections are steep and exposed—the consequences of a fall could be very serious. After exiting the cliffs, cross the Alpine Garden Trail. Continue to **Nelson Crag Trail** and follow this to the summit. Descend via Lion Head or Tuckerman Ravine.

8–10 hours, 8.4 miles, elevation gain: 4,270'

Approach: Start on the Tuckerman Ravine Trail from Pinkham Notch.

Mount Washington via Nelson Crag

This is a longer and less-travelled route up Washington. From Pinkham Notch, follow **Old Jackson Road** (the Appalachian Trail, or AT) for 1.7 miles (after briefly coinciding with Raymond Path) before heading left up **Nelson Crag Trail**. After about an hour (1.5 miles), you'll graze the Auto Road at a hairpin turn and continue in the open to the top of Nelson Crag at 5,635'. At first paralleling the Auto Road, the trail eventually crosses it and the Cog Railway, reaching the summit 5 miles from Pinkham Notch. Descend the Lion Head Trail or Tuckerman Ravine Trail.

9 hours, 9 miles, elevation gain: 4,400'

Glen Boulder

Glen Boulder is a large boulder precariously perched 2,000' above Route 16. You can see it on the left, high on the mountainside, as you drive up to Pinkham Notch from Jackson. The hike to the boulder is a moderately demanding climb; the trail is steep and rough. The boulder is above treeline, thus there are excellent views. **Glen Boulder Trail** continues up the mountain 1.6 miles, ending at Davis Path. From here it is 2.5 miles (head right) to the top of Mount Washington on the Davis and Crawford Paths. One can then descend to Pinkham Notch via Tuckerman Ravine, Lion Head, or Boott Spur, making a full day of it.

3 hours, 3 miles, elevation gain: 1,780' (Glen Boulder only)

Approach: Start from the parking area for Glen Ellis Falls, 0.8 mile south of Pinkham Notch Visitor Center on NH 16.

3-Day Loop Hike from Pinkham Notch

Day 1: Pinkham Notch to Madison Hut

Follow the white-blazed **Old Jackson Road** (the AT) as it climbs through woods, at times steeply, reaching the Auto Road at 1.9 miles. Cross the road; the trail is now the **Madison Gulf Trail**. Pass the spur trail to Lowe's Bald Spot—jog right for the famous view—and descend 600' into **Great Gulf**, a federally designated wilderness area. Bear right on the Great Gulf Trail, and cross the river. After passing Madison Gulf Trail (left), head left on **Osgood Cutoff** to reach the **Osgood Trail**. Follow this, climbing above treeline, reaching the summit of **Mount Madison** (5,367') at 7.5 miles. From here it's about a half hour down to Madison Hut. Note: This entire day, and the next, are on the Appalachian Trail.

8 hours, 8 miles, elevation gain: 3,850'

Day 2: Madison Hut to Lakes of the Clouds Hut

From Madison Hut, follow the **Gulfside Trail** as it winds its way among, but not over, the higher summits of the Northern Presidentials: You can easily do side trips to the summits of Adams and Jefferson—see the map. **Thunderstorm Junction** is reached at 0.9 mile and **Edmands Col** at 2.2 miles. The loop over Jefferson summit adds only 250' of climbing. After passing **Mt. Clay** and the top of spectacular **Great Gulf**, you reach the top of **Mount Washington** at 6 miles. From here, descend on **Crawford Path** the remaining 1.5 miles to Lakes of the Clouds Hut at 5,010'. Above treeline for its entire length, this is a spectacular route in fine weather, but do not attempt it if the weather is questionable. Know the various "escape routes." All members of your party must have adequate storm clothing.

5–6 hours, 7.5 miles, elev. gain: 2,600' (Gulfside Trail only)

Day 3: Lakes of the Clouds to Pinkham Notch

From Lakes of the Clouds follow **Tuckerman Crossover** across open, weather-exposed terrain to **Tuckerman Junction**, climbing and descending about 500' in the process. Now continue on the

Tuckerman Ravine Trail, making the very steep descent of the Headwall into the Ravine, down to Hermit Lake shelters and the protection of the forest. From here, it is an easy, if somewhat rocky 2.4 miles down to Pinkham Notch on the heavily-travelled lower portion of Tuckerman Ravine Trail.

3–4 hours, 4.6 miles, elevation gain: 500', elevation loss: 3,500'

Maps: AMC: #1 *Presidential Range;* DeLorme; Map Adventures: *White Mountains Hiking;* Washburn (AMC): *Mount Washington and the Heart of the Presidential Range;* Wilderness Map Co.: *Mt. Washington.*

Camping: *The Dolly Copp Campground (Forest Service) is a few miles north of Pinkham Notch, and Moose Brook State Park is in Gorham. The lean-to shelters at Hermit Lake are available year round. There are private campgrounds in North Conway, Bartlett, Shelburne, and Berlin.*

Treeline and Arctic Vegetation

Alpine environments are characterized by a well-defined transition from forested to barren slopes determined by elevation, climate and latitude. The upper reaches of Mount Washington and its neighboring peaks are treeless and rocky; they seem to be devoid of life, yet a large variety of fragile plants is native to this harsh environment. The 8-square mile area on Washington is by far the largest arctic zone in the eastern United States. The transition to the alpine zone, also called the arctic–alpine zone, is signaled by a brief band of stunted, wind-contorted spruces—an abrupt termination of the forest zone. Immediately above this "treeline," arctic plants nestle among the rocks. In the severe climate of the White Mountains, arctic vegetation can appear as low as 4,500'. The various grasses and flowers that thrive here are easily damaged by foot traffic—recovery can take years. Amazingly, some of the plants need 25 years to bloom for the first time! Hikers are thus urged to stay on the trail, and to step only on rocks.

1B Great Gulf

The largest cirque in the White Mountains, Great Gulf is a magnificent glacial valley that begins just north of Mount Washington's summit—it plunges downward only a few yards from the Cog Railway tracks. At the foot of the headwall lies tiny, secluded Spaulding Lake. Below the lake, the wall formed by Jefferson, Adams, and Madison forms the left side of the cirque, as the valley widens and curves to the east. Six miles from its beginning it merges with the main drainage off Pinkham Notch. From below, looking into Great Gulf from Route 16, the wild, densely forested basin rimmed by rugged mountains is an imposing sight.

Mount Washington via Great Gulf Trail

With waterfalls, a rushing stream, and a gentle woods stroll giving way to an arduous climb along huge boulders, this trip changes texture many times before yielding to the splendor of high-altitude Spaulding Lake and Mount Washington, 1,500' above. From highway-side parking, beginning on an old logging road and crossing the west branch of the Peabody River on wooden foot bridges, the Great Gulf Trail enters the **Great Gulf Wilderness** at 1.7 miles. From here it works its way up the base of the ravine, passing several good swimming spots and rocks for sunning. From the highway the 2.7 miles (pass the Osgood Trail) to the Osgood Cutoff make for easy, low-angle walking. Continuing, cross the Madison Gulf Trail, then Chandler Brook Trail, and finally reach the rugged Six Husbands Trail (right) and Wamsutta Trail (left) at 4.5 miles. Above, there are beautiful cascades, a fine waterfall, and great views down into the Gulf. Continue, and after passing the Sphinx Trail (right) at 5.6 miles; you reach **Spaulding Lake** (4,250') at 6.5 miles. From here the trail tackles the 1,500'-headwall in a direct fashion, topping out at the **Gulfside Trail**, a half mile from the summit. Take the Gulfside Trail the rest of the way. Descend by the same route or via the Wamsutta Trail (below). Climbing Washington via Great Gulf makes for a very long day; see the end of this section for Great Gulf camping information.

Great Gulf   Jared Gange

10–12 hours, 15.6 miles, elevation gain: 5,050'
Approach: *From the base of the Auto Road, drive north 1.6 miles to the parking area for the Great Gulf Trail.*

Wamsutta and Chandler Brook variation:

After ascending the lower portion of Great Gulf, branch left (at 4 miles) on the one-mile **Chandler Brook Trail** and climb steeply to reach the **Auto Road**. After a short stretch on the road, bear right on the more direct "Winter Cut-off", and after meeting the road again, cross it and continue on **Alpine Garden Trail** to **Nelson Crag Trail**. Head right on Nelson Crag Trail, reaching the summit after another 700' of climbing. Descend by the same route, but depart left from the Winter Cut-off on **Wamsutta Trail** (instead of Chandler Brook Trail) to return to Great Gulf. From here it is 4.5 miles back to Route 16 on the Great Gulf Trail.

10 hours, 15.4 miles, total climb: 5,050' (to summit)

Mt. Madison: Madison Gulf and Osgood Trails

A mile-long above-treeline approach to Madison's summit makes this an exciting and unique foray into a world of boulders, arctic vegetation, and sweeping views. If coming in June, you'll see alpine azaleas and diapensia in bloom. The top of Madison, a rocky climb, brings you to a breathtaking panorama of the area; Washington rises majestically in the distance. From the trailhead, cross the suspension bridge and head left on the **Great Gulf Trail** over gentle terrain. At 1.7 miles turn right on the Osgood Trail, climbing easily at first, then in earnest, after passing the Osgood Cut-off (your return route). The last mile of the Osgood Trail on the approach to Madison's summit is above treeline. As always, the dramatic, sweeping views mean potential exposure to wind and storms, so pay attention to the weather. From the summit (5,367'), descend on rocks (still the Osgood Trail) to **Madison Hut** at 4,809', where snacks (nothing elaborate) can usually be purchased. Leaving the hut, head 0.1 mile on the **Star Lake Trail** across the tundra to the **Parapet Trail** before branching right onto **Madison Gulf Trail** to descend the cirque of Madison Gulf. The 1½-hour descent alternates between steep and moderate sections. After completing this long descent, turn left on Great Gulf Trail and continue on it back to your starting point.

8 hours, 11.5 miles, total climb: 4,040'

Approach: Great Gulf trailhead is 1.6 miles north of the Auto Road.

Mount Madison via Daniel Webster Scout Trail

This is a convenient route up Madison for folks camping at Dolly Copp. The Daniel Webster Scout Trail climbs pleasantly through the woods (3 miles) before abruptly emerging from the trees to climb a steep slope of loose rock, meeting the **Osgood Trail** 3.5 miles from the campground. From here—Osgood Junction—it is about a half mile across interesting open terrain to the summit of Mount Madison. Return by the same route.

6½ hours, 8.2 miles, total climb: 4,120'

Approach: Start at the south end of Dolly Copp Campground. (See map).

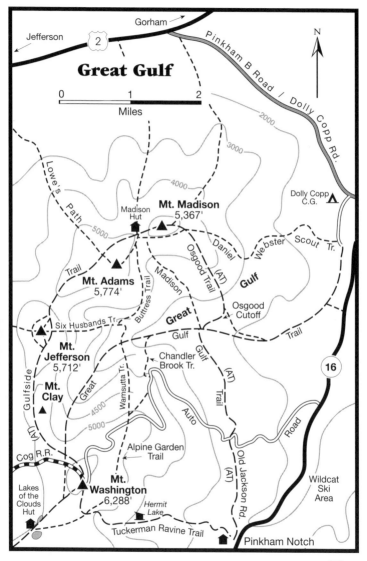

Great Gulf

0   1   2

Miles

N

Jefferson

Gorham

Pinkham B Road / Dolly Copp Rd.

2000

3000

4000

5000

Lowe's Path

Trail

Madison Hut

Mt. Madison
5,367'

Dolly Copp C.G.

Daniel

Webster

Scout Tr.

Osgood Trail (AT)

Mt. Adams
5,774'

Buttress Trail

Madison

Gulf

Osgood
Cutoff

Six Husbands Tr.

Great

Gulf

Trail

Mt.
Jefferson
5,712'

Gulfside (AT)

Great

Wamsutta Tr.

Chandler
Brook Tr.

Gulf (AT) Trail

Mt. Clay

4500

5000

Auto

16

Cog R.R.

Alpine Garden
Trail

Mt.
Washington
6,288'

Old Jackson Rd. (AT)

Road

Wildcat
Ski
Area

Lakes
of the
Clouds
Hut

Hermit
Lake

Tuckerman Ravine Trail

Pinkham Notch

Mt. Jefferson (5,712') via Six Husbands Trail

The top-of-the-world feeling and the views into the upper Gulf from the Six Husbands Trail are fantastic! Hike up **Great Gulf Trail** 4.5 miles to the junction of the Wamsutta and Six Husband Trails, a good area for a campsite. Head right on Six Husbands Trail which soon becomes extremely steep. After toiling up past some huge boulders in the dense forest, the trail resorts to ladders in two places. Without these, a hiking route would not be possible. The gradient eventually eases, and after crossing the Gulfside Trail, reach the summit after 7 miles and about 5 hours from the road.

For variety and a less demanding return route, consider descending via the somewhat easier, but steep and rough **Sphinx Trail**, as follows. From the top, walk south (toward Mt. Washington) for 0.3 mile on **Jefferson Loop** to **Gulfside Trail**, and continue 0.6 mile to Sphinx Col, where the Sphinx Trail descends to the left. At times you walk directly in a rocky stream bed, or pass near several fine waterfalls. The sound of running water is within earshot most of the time. Be careful on the wet rocks, and allow yourself plenty of time for this difficult trail. After climbing down 1,400' (1.1 miles), head left on Great Gulf Trail. It is 5.6 miles back to the trailhead and highway; you pass the junction with the Six Husbands Trail after about a mile.

10 hours, 14.5 miles, total climb: 4,460' (loop version)
Approach: From the Great Gulf trailhead parking on NH 16.

Alternate return via Great Gulf Headwall

Those with the extra time and energy may want to continue south from Jefferson's summit across **Mount Clay** (5,533') and over to the top of the 1,500'-headwall of Great Gulf, a distance of 1.7 miles. The headwall, although higher than Tuckerman Ravine's headwall, does not reach its steepness. From the top of the headwall it is 7.5 miles down the Great Gulf Trail to NH 16 and the trailhead. Of course, once at the top of the headwall, it is only a short half mile and a climb of 300' to the top of Mount Washington—a short detour certainly worth considering, if time and weather are in agreement.

Spaulding Lake in Great Gulf   Robert Kozlow

Maps: AMC: *#1 Presidential Range;* DeLorme; Map Adventures: *White Mountains Hiking;* Washburn: *Mt. Washington and the Heart of the Presidential Range;* Wilderness Map Co.: *Mt. Washington.*

Camping in the Great Gulf Wilderness:

Most of Great Gulf is a designated wilderness, and hikers must observe the usage regulations. The Forest Service continually monitors these "Forest Protection Areas" for signs of overuse. Camping is permitted at established tent sites and elsewhere in Great Gulf, except as noted: Not above treeline, nor within 200 feet of a stream, trail, or road, nor on frozen lakes or ponds. Camping is not permitted above the Sphinx Trail junction. If campers are not using one of the established campsites, they are required to camp at least a quarter mile from shelters or tent sites. Groups may not be larger than ten. No open fires are allowed—use portable stoves. Refer to the info boxes on pages 97 and 99 for more information. Campers should obtain a copy of the current backcountry camping rules from a Ranger Station or the Appalachian Mountain Club.

Mount Washington Auto Road

The historic Mount Washington Auto Road begins at Glen House on Route 16, two miles north of Wildcat Ski Area and about three miles north of Pinkham Notch Visitor Center. Completed in 1861, this mostly gravel road zigzags for 7.6 miles up the northeast shoulder of Mt. Washington, to just below the summit. The upper half of the drive is breathtaking. Despite the terrific views, some may find the steep and barren mountainside an unlikely place for a road. There is a "stage service" for those who would rather not drive themselves; cars and motorcycles pay a toll. Hiking is allowed, although the road is more significant for foot traffic in the winter than in summer. Several hiking trails cross or make contact with the road, including the Appalachian Trail. Annual events include a running race in the spring and a bike race in the fall. Some hikers may find the Auto Road to be a negative presence, but for those unable to hike, it provides an exciting glimpse of a unique and precious environment. And who knows how many people have been turned on to mountains by a chance drive up the Auto Road? The history of the Auto Road and the summit weather observatory (manned year round) is quite interesting and well-documented: There are excellent displays and a small museum in the summit building. And last but not least, the cafeteria and gift shops are enjoyed by all: those that arrive by cog railway, by car and on foot.

1c   The Carter Range

Across the highway from Mount Washington, the Carter Range is the steep mountainside which forms the east wall of Pinkham Notch. The well-defined ridge, with six summits over 4,000', runs north to the Androscoggin River, which cuts through the range a few miles east of Gorham. North of the river the continuation of the range is known as the Mahoosuc Range. Wildcat Mountain forms the southern end of the Carter Range; it juts high above the road, across from the Pinkham Notch Visitor Center. The Appalachian Trail ascends this buttress, traverses Wildcat Mountain's summits, drops into wild Carter Notch, and continues north along the main ridgeline to Route 2. Along the way, various side trails ascend the ridge from NH 16 on the west and from the Wild River Valley on the east.

Mount Hight and Carter Dome (4,832')

Carter Dome is the major peak of the range, but nearby Mount Hight (4,675') has a better view. For a good loop trip across both summits, start out on **Nineteen Mile Brook Trail**. After ascending along a pleasant stream, branch left onto **Carter Dome Trail**, reaching Zeta Pass on the main ridge at 3.8 miles. Now head 1.2 miles south (right) on the **Carter-Moriah Trail** to Carter Dome, traversing Mt. Hight along the way (Hight's summit can be bypassed). Beyond Carter Dome, descend steeply to the two ponds that nestle in **Carter Notch**, passing the Sentinel (a huge boulder) after about a mile. From the notch, the short side trip (left) to **Carter Notch Hut** is worthwhile. There is bunk space for 40, and staff is on hand year round. The original stone portion of the hut dates from 1914. Leaving the hut, hike back past the ponds on Nineteen Mile Brook Trail, make the short, steep climb to the notch proper, and descend the 3.6 miles back to NH 16. The trail drops steeply at first, then eases lower down.

7 hours, 10.2 miles, total climb: 3,400'

Approach: *From Pinkham Notch drive north 3.5 miles to parking for the Nineteen Mile Brook Trail, on the right.*

Carter Notch Hut & Caretaker   Jared Gange

Carter Notch Hut from Jackson

From the end of Carter Notch Road, follow **Bog Brook Trail** for 0.7 mile, then head left on **Wildcat River Trail** for 3.6 miles to the hut. Longer than Nineteen Mile Brook Trail's western approach, this route's gentle gradient makes it a better choice for skiers. For information on winter activity, see Backcountry Skiing.

4½ hours, 8.6 miles round trip, total climb: 1,730'

Wild River Valley from Jackson

Above the village of Jackson, at the end of Carter Notch Road, the **Bog Brook Trail** leads to the **Wild River Trail**, which then heads though **Perkins Notch** and into the Wild River Valley. From here you can continue to the Wild River Campground or, by ascending **Eagle Link**, gain the main ridge of the Baldface Range, just north of **the Baldfaces** (3,591'). See Evans Notch (Chapter 7) for the main approach to these mountains.

Traversing the Wildcat Range from Pinkham

Head north on the Appalachian Trail past Lost Pond to the **Wildcat Ridge Trail** at 0.9 mile. Here, begin a prolonged steep climb—about 2 hours—to Wildcat E, the first of the five alphabetically named summits of Wildcat Mountain. Several fine ledges with great views of Mt. Washington sweeten the climb. Continue, passing the ski area gondola, and climb up to the observation platform on **Wildcat D** (4,070'), where there are again excellent views. Traverse the ridge, passing through shallow cols and occasional swampy areas, crossing over "C" and "B", and finally reaching **Wildcat A**, at 4,422' the highest point. Of the Wildcat summits, only "D" and "A" are official 4,000'-ers. From Wildcat A, the view into Carter Notch is dramatic. Descend steeply into the notch, where the side trip (0.2 mile right) past two tarns to **Carter Notch Hut** is worth the extra effort. The return to NH 16 via **Nineteen Mile Brook Trail** is an enjoyable 3.8-mile descent.

7½ hours, 9.7 miles, total climb: 2,800'

Appalachian Mountain Club

The AMC, the primary hiking organization in New England, is a recreation and conservation group with over 80,000 members. In addition to hiking, activities include canoeing, skiing, rock climbing, and bicycling. The AMC offers classes in everything from introductory camping to mountain leadership skills. The Club's regional chapters oversee the maintenance of 1,200 miles of trails. Open to the public and conveniently spaced along the Appalachian Trail the AMC's eight European-style huts provide shelter, bunks, and meals. The AMC's Pinkham Notch Visitor Center (Pinkham Notch Camp), at the base of Mt. Washington and on the Appalachian Trail, is a mecca for hikers and skiers. The AMC also operates a shuttle which transports hikers between trailheads. By joining the AMC you participate in the stewardship of our natural areas and help to foster environmentally sound recreation activities.

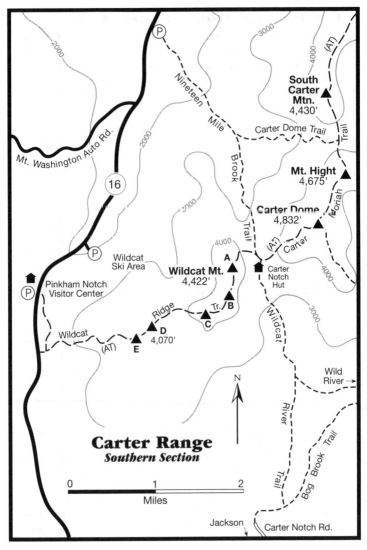

Carter Range
Southern Section

0   1   2
Miles

Imp Face and Middle Carter 4,610'

The **Imp Trail** forms a kind of loop, the northern arm of which leads to the top of prominent Imp Face (3,165') 2.2 miles from the highway. From the cliff there is an immediate view of the Northern Presies, and Imp Brook is nestled in its ravine 1,000' directly below. The trail then heads south, to meet **North Carter Trail**. This in turn leads (left) to the main ridge and the **Carter-Moriah Trail**, at a point between North and Middle Carter, at 4.3 miles. Turn right here, passing across **Mount Lethe** (better views than from Middle Carter) to reach the top of Middle Carter (15th highest) after 0.6 mile. Peakbaggers can continue south another 1.3 miles to **South Carter** (at 4,430', 20th highest). From Middle Carter, return to Imp Trail the way you came. Head left at the Imp Trail for variety; it's only 0.3 mile farther, counting the 0.2-mile road segment that joins the south and north arms of the loop.

7 hours, 10.2 miles, total climb: 3,320' (Middle Carter)
Approach: The northern Imp trailhead is on NH 16, 2.6 miles north of the Mt. Washington Auto Road.

Mount Moriah 4,049'

From NH 16 follow **Stony Brook Trail** for 3.5 miles as it climbs 2,200' to reach **Carter-Moriah Trail.** The first two thirds are moderately graded, with the final section rockier and fairly steep. Now on the main ridge, head left on Carter-Moriah for the final 1.4 miles and 900' of climbing—much of it on fun, south-facing ledges with plunging views into the Wild River Valley—to the top of Mount Moriah. The flat, open summit affords panoramic views of the Mahoosucs, the Androscoggin River Valley, the Northern Presidentials, and south along the Carter Range.

6½ hours, 10 miles, total climb: 3,100'
Approach: The trailhead is on NH 16, two miles south of Gorham (and six miles north of the Auto Road), on the east side of the highway.

Note: Just on the other side of the ridge from Stony Brook Trail, **Moriah Brook Trail** descends through beautiful woods into **Wild River Valley**, the valley between the Baldface and Carter Ranges.

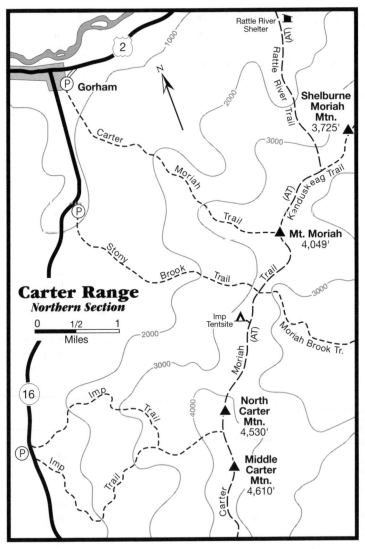

Carter Range
Northern Section

0   1/2   1
Miles

Rattle River
Shelter

Shelburne
Moriah
Mtn.
3,725'

Mt. Moriah
4,049'

Imp
Tentsite

North
Carter
Mtn.
4,530'

Middle
Carter
Mtn.
4,610'

Gorham

Carter

Moriah

Trail

Stony

Brook   Trail

Rattle River Trail

(AT)

Kenduskeag Trail

Moriah Brook Tr.

Moriah

(AT)

Imp

Trail

Imp   Trail

Carter

1000

2000

3000

3000

2000

3000

4000

Shelburne Moriah 3,725'

It is not surprising that Shelburne Moriah, positioned at the northern end of the range, is one of the best viewpoints along the entire ridge. The view north to the Mahoosucs, the Androscoggin Valley, Mount Madison and the Northern Presidentials make this a beautiful spot. From the trailhead on Route 2, follow the **Rattle River Trail** (AT) past the shelter (1.7 miles), reaching the **Kenduskeag Trail** at 4.3 miles, after about 3 hours. Head left on the Kenduskeag Trail for 1.3 miles to the large open summit. Return by the same route.

> *7 hours, 11.2 miles, total climb: 3,000'*
> *Approach: The trailhead is on US 2, 3.5 miles east of Gorham, on the south side of the road.*

Variations: The detour following the Kenduskeag Trail south to **Mount Moriah** (4,049', 41st highest) and then back via the Rattle River Trail adds about 1½ hours and 2.8 miles to the above trip. Alternately, descending directly from Mt. Moriah to Gorham on the Carter–Moriah Trail makes for a trip of 7½ hours and 11.5 miles, and leaves a short road stretch for which you will need to organize transportation.

Complete Traverse of the Carter Range

From Pinkham Notch the hike north along the Carter Range to Gorham (or Route 2) can be done as a three-day trip. The 5-mile section on the **Wildcat Ridge Trail** to **Carter Notch Hut** makes a reasonable first day. (See the descriptions for Wildcat and the other individual hikes.) On day two (7.5 miles), continue north from the hut on the **Carter-Moriah Trail** over Carter Dome, South, Middle, and North Carter to **Imp Campsite** (side trail left 2 miles past N. Carter Tr.). Third day (7 miles): hike over Mount Moriah and down to Gorham on the final section of the Carter-Moriah Trail.

> *3 days, 19.5 miles, total climbing: 6,800'*
> *Approach: Start from Pinkham Notch Visitor Center on Route 16.*

Maps: AMC: #5 Carter Range-Evans Notch; DeLorme; Map Adventures: *White Mountains Trail Map, White Mountains Hiking*; USGS: *Carter Dome, Jackson, and Wild River.*

1D Pinkham Notch Short Hikes

As a starting point for hiking on Mount Washington, and for skiers who want to test themselves in Tuckerman Ravine, Pinkham Notch is not associated with gentle terrain. But there is a good selection of short hikes suitable for families with small children, or for those who want pleasant walks of a mile or two. In this section we give an introduction to the trails in the vicinity of Pinkham Notch Visitor Center. Nearby Wildcat Ski Area provides another option: Ride up on the gondola, make the short climb to the observation platform on Wildcat "D," and walk down the ski runs—the views are spectacular.

Crystal Cascade

Crystal Cascade is an attractive little waterfall on the way up Mount Washington. From Pinkham Notch Visitor Center start out on the **Tuckerman Ravine Trail**. After a short distance the trail swings left, crosses the river, and climbs past the viewpoint for Crystal Cascade on the right. Return the same way.

1 hour (or less), 0.8 mile, total climb: 200'

For those up for a longer hike, it is another 2 miles (and 1,700' of climbing) to the interesting **Hermit Lake** area where there are shelters and good views of Boott Spur and the steep slopes of the upper mountain. There are no views until Hermit Lake (3,860').

Liebeskind's Loop

This is a loop of moderate length with some interesting views. From the Visitor Center follow **Old Jackson Road** 0.3 mile and turn right on **Crew Cut**. Stay on Crew Cut for about 0.7 mile (passing George's Gorge Trail after crossing a stream) until you reach Liebeskind's Loop. Head left, up past Lila's Ledge (300' detour right to a view) to Casey's Cliff, which has excellent views. To complete the loop, continue to **George's Gorge Trail** (head left), and follow it back down to Crew Cut. Turn right here and return to Old Jackson Road; turn left to walk back to the Visitor Center.

1½ hours, 2.3 miles, total climb: 700'

Crystal Cascade on the Tuckerman Ravine Trail
Bob Grant

Lowe's Bald Spot 2,875'

There are good views to the north and of Great Gulf from Lowe's Bald Spot. Start out on **Tuckerman Ravine Trail**, branching right onto white-blazed **Old Jackson Road** (AT southbound) after 200 feet. Continue on Old Jackson Road to the **Mt. Washington Auto Road** at about 2 miles. Cross the road and continue on the AT, now the **Madison Gulf Trail**. After a short distance, pick up a side trail (right) and clamber (for 0.1 mile) up to the ledgy, open "summit" that is Lowe's Bald Spot. Return by the same route. Since Lowe's Bald Spot is in a wilderness area, wilderness usage rules apply.

2½ hours, 4.4 miles, total climb: 900'

Lost Pond

From the AMC parking lot at Pinkham Notch, cross the highway and pick up **Lost Pond Trail**. It crosses Cutler River and heads south, paralleling the river over easy ground. At about 0.4 mile you will come to the northern end of the pond. Follow the trail along the pond's east side, where there are good views of Mount Washington. Continue to the southern end of the pond to see a wild jumble of large boulders. Return by the same route.

30–60 minutes, 1.2 miles, total climb: 50'

For a longer hike, follow Lost Pond Trail south to the **Wildcat Ridge Trail** and make the very steep climb up Wildcat Mountain, crossing various clfftop ledges. At about 1.5 miles there is a stunning view across Pinkham Notch to Mount Washington.

Square Ledge

Considered to have one of the better views in the White Mountains, Square Ledge makes a great short hike. Start out as for Lost Pond (above) but immediately after crossing the river branch left on the **Square Ledge Trail** (blue blazes). Follow this up a steep bank. The trail climbs moderately, crosses the **Square Ledge Ski Trail**, and soon passes **Hangover Rock**. After reaching the base of Square Ledge itself, climb steeply to the top with its sweeping view of Mount Washington and Tuckerman Ravine.

45–60 minutes, 1.2 miles, total climb: 400'

Glen Ellis Falls

With its 70' drop, Glen Ellis Falls is the highest waterfall in the area. It marks the beginning of the Cutler River's descent from the notch into the valley. From the parking lot, take the pedestrian walkway under the highway and follow the well-engineered stone pathway down to the pool at the base of the waterfall.

20-30 minutes round trip
Approach: The falls are 0.7 mile south of the Visitor Center.

Maps: AMC: *#1 Presidential Range;* Map Adventures; Washburn: *Mt. Washington;* Pinkham Notch; Wilderness Map Company.

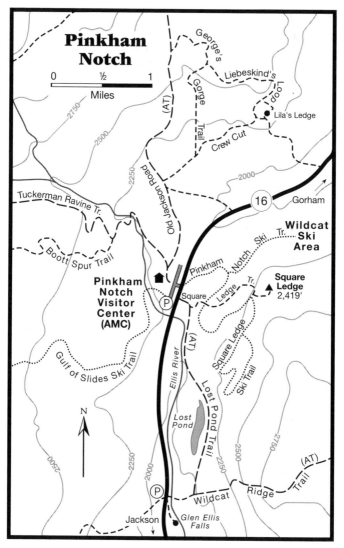

Pinkham Notch

0   ½   1
Miles

George's

Liebeskind's Loop

Lila's Ledge

(AT)

Gorge Trail

Crew Cut

Old Jackson Road

2750

2500

2250

2000

16   Gorham

Tuckerman Ravine Tr.

Wildcat Ski Area

Boott Spur Trail

Pinkham Notch Ski Tr.

Square Ledge 2,419'

Pinkham Notch Visitor Center (AMC)

P

Square Ledge Tr.

Pinkham

(AT)

Square Ledge Ski Trail

Gulf of Slides Ski Trail

Ellis River

N

Lost Pond Trail

Lost Pond

2250

2500

2750

(AT)

P

Wildcat Ridge Trail

Jackson   Glen Ellis Falls

2500

2000

Pinkham Notch Visitor Center

Pinkham Notch Visitor Center, formerly known as Pinkham Notch Camp, is the most important trailhead on Mt. Washington and in New England. As the trailhead for Tuckerman Ravine, 2.4 miles away, Pinkham is a beehive of activity year round. Operated by the AMC under permit from the Forest Service, the facility offers food, lodging, and hiking information. It is also a center for workshops, seminars, and evening lectures. The hikers' store sells guide books, maps, and various supplies, while the dining room and a 24-hour locker room with showers are especially appreciated by AT through-hikers. AMC staff is on hand to offer advice on trip planning. Across the courtyard from the Visitor Center, the Joe Dodge Lodge has accommodations for more than 100 guests. The trails described in this chapter are part of the network of shorter trails in the immediate vicinity of Pinkham Notch. Several cross country ski trails originate from the Visitor Center.

Pinkham Notch from Square Ledge   Jared Gange

2 Mount Washington From The West

As seen from the fields of Bretton Woods, Mount Washington and the Southern Presidentials—the long, high ridge to the right of Washington—form an imposing mountain wall that ends at Crawford Notch. Most of the hiking routes given in this section start from the parking area a short distance below the Cog Railway Base Station, about 5 miles from US 302. The popular Ammonoosuc Ravine Trail to Lakes of the Clouds Hut starts from here and is the standard route up Washington from the west. Edmands Path on Mt. Eisenhower is another classic. When approaching from the south on I-93, take exit 35, follow US 3 to Twin Mountain, and turn right on US 302 to Bretton Woods.

Mt. Washington via Ammonoosuc Ravine Trail

This interesting and very popular trail climbs—at times seemingly straight up—to the AMC's **Lakes of the Clouds Hut** (5,010'). After a rocky but gentle beginning the trail climbs more briskly and reaches attractive **Gem Pool** at 2.1 miles. From this point, the trail is extremely steep in places, but the footing is good, and there is usually something to hang on to. You'll pass several viewpoints—followed by stream crossings on rock slabs—before emerging from the woods just below the hut (3.1 miles). At the level of the hut, you are in a treeless arctic world of rocks and wind. Take a moment to evaluate the weather before continuing. Mt. Monroe is nearby, and to the north the summit of Mount Washington beckons, 1.4 miles away and 1,200' higher. To continue, head north on **Crawford Path** and stay on it to the top (about an hour). At the beginning of the final, rocky climb up the barren summit cone, Davis Path enters from the right, and immediately thereafter the Westside Trail enters from the left. Descend the same route.

7–8 hours, 8.8 miles, total climb: 3,800'

Approach: *The trailhead parking lot is on the Base Road, 5.5 miles from Bretton Woods and US 302.*

Mount Monroe and Lakes of the Clouds Hut   Robert Kozlow

Mount Monroe 5,384'

Hike up the Ammonoosuc Ravine Trail, as described above. From Lakes of the Clouds Hut, follow **Crawford Path** 0.1 mile south to **Monroe Loop**, and complete the 360' climb to the top. There are excellent views in all directions from the bare summit, especially of Mount Washington, only 1.4 miles distant. Although insignificant next to Mount Washington, Mount Monroe is a summit in its own right—4th highest in New Hampshire. It makes a good fallback option if Mount Washington does not work out. Well above treeline, it is very exposed to the elements. Avoid being caught here in bad weather. With normal conditions, it takes about an hour to make the climb and return to the hut. The round trip distance from the hut is 0.8 mile.

5 hours, 7 miles, elevation gain: 2,900'

Approach: Start from the hiker parking area, 0.4 mile below the Cog Railway Base Station.

The Jewell Trail up Mount Washington

Starting across the road from Ammonoosuc Ravine Trail parking area, the Jewell Trail climbs at a pleasant grade on an excellent path and ends on the **Gulfside Trail**, a little north of Clay Col. From here, it is 1.4 miles right (south) on Gulfside Trail to the summit of Washington, for a total distance of 5 miles. The trail skirts the top of **Great Gulf's** 1,500' headwall, and provides you with an impressive view down this glacial valley. Cross the tracks of the Cog RR about 0.4 mile from the top, then head left onto **Crawford Path** for the final few minutes to the summit. During the summer and fall season, this is a busy place. It's all here: cafeteria, restrooms, museum, and souvenir shops. Descend by the same route, or see the **Ammonoosuc Ravine Trail** variation, below.

7 hours, 10 miles, elevation gain: 3,650'
Approach: From Bretton Woods, take the Base Road for 5 miles to the hiker parking area on the right.

Ammonoosuc Ravine and Jewell Trail Loop

For an interesting loop hike, ascend Washington via Ammonoosuc Ravine and Crawford Path as described above, and descend on the Gulfside Trail and Jewell Trail. This gives you the dramatic views into Great Gulf, and walking down the Jewell Trail is much more relaxing than the steepness of the Ammonoosuc Ravine Trail. This is a classic circuit. See above for more detail on each trail segment.

Totals: 7–8 hours, 9.6 miles, elevation climbed: 3,800'
Approach: Start and finish at the hiker parking area, 0.4 mile below the Cog Railway Base Station.

Mount Eisenhower (4,760') via Edmands Path

This classic hike starts a few miles north of Crawford Notch on Mt. Clinton Road. Viewed from Bretton Woods, Eisenhower is a graceful, rounded peak—it's the last distinctive mountain of the Presidential ridge before Crawford Notch. From the parking area, climb on Edmands Path as it ascends moderately, passing the tree-line at 2.8 miles. At 3 miles, bear right on **Eisenhower Loop** and scramble up steep ledges to the top (3.4 miles). With its constant

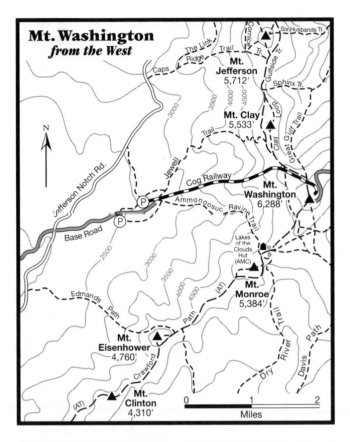

Mt. Washington
from the West

Mt. Jefferson 5,712'

Mt. Clay 5,533'

Mt. Washington 6,288'

Mt. Monroe 5,384'

Mt. Eisenhower 4,760'

Mt. Clinton 4,310'

Lakes of the Clouds Hut (AMC)

Cog Railway

Base Road

Jefferson Notch Rd.

Edmands Path

Six Husbands Tr.

N

0   1   2
Miles

angle of ascent and careful stone paving and cribbing, the historic Edmands Path is one of the more carefully engineered trails in the state. From the top, only the mass of Mount Washington interrupts the panorama—it looms three miles away as the raven flies.

Totals: 5 hours, 6.8 miles, climbing: 2,730'

Approach: *Park on Mt. Clinton Road, 1.3 miles south of the Base Road, or about 2.3 miles north of US 302.*

Mount Washington Cog Railway

Mount Washington's historic Cog Railway is the world's oldest mountain-climbing railway. It began service in 1869 when Ulysses Grant was president. The 2.8-mile line climbs 3,600' to the top of the mountain. On spectacular Jacob's Ladder, a 300'-long curving trestle, the gradient reaches 37%, making it the second steepest passenger railway in the world. Only Mount Pilatus in Switzerland is steeper.

With a unique locomotive design adapted to existing cog technology, New Hampshire businessman and inventor Sylvester Marsh devised a propulsion system capable of handling Mount Washington's steep slopes. Although they have been overhauled many times, the original coal-fired steam engines are still used to transport thousands of people up the mountain every summer.

Photo: Jared Gange

Mount Jefferson (5,712') and the Ridge of Caps

Jefferson is the next major summit to the north of Mt. Washington, and its distinctive west ridge—the Ridge of Caps—is the classic route. Starting from 3,000' Jefferson Notch, the **Caps Ridge Trail** quickly brings you above treeline and onto the exposed, rocky ridge leading to the summit. Several very steep sections (the "caps") and the rough boulder field near the summit area make the route challenging. After leaving the parking area, you pass the **Link** (left) at 1.1 miles. (See the loop variation described below.) From 1.5 miles to the Cornice Trail at 2.1 miles, the trail is steep and difficult as you negotiate the various caps. At 2.5 miles you reach the open summit with its stunning views of Adams and Washington. As always, be prepared for wind and lower temperatures on the summit, and keep a close eye on the weather, as a good portion of this route is above treeline. And the rough nature of the trail on the upper mountain is not conducive to a quick scamper back down to safety! Return by the same route, or by the following detour; it adds a mile and gives a fuller perspective of the high mountain terrain. Take **Jefferson Loop** south off the summit to **Gulfside Trail**. Stay right, soon reaching the **Cornice Trail**. Follow this (right) for 0.5 mile to the Caps Ridge Trail, and descend on it—the way you came up—to Jefferson Notch.

4¼ hours, 5 miles, total climb: 2,700'

Approach: From Bretton Woods, drive 4.5 miles up Base Road to Jefferson Notch Road and proceed (left) 3.3 miles to Jefferson Notch and the trailhead parking. Note: Jefferson Notch Road is not plowed in winter.

Castle Trail variation: By hiking the Link (a rough trail) for 2.5 miles to reach the **Castle Trail**, and then climbing steeply, clambering up and around the "castles" as you negotiate the **Castellated Ridge**, you obtain an interesting variation on the regular Ridge of Caps route. The view down into **Castle Ravine** is *impressive*. From the summit, descend the **Caps Ridge Trail** to Jefferson Notch. This variation is an hour and 2.5 miles longer than the normal up-and-back route.

Mount Jefferson to Mount Washington

Heading south from Jefferson's summit on Jefferson Loop and the Gulfside Trail takes one across 3.6 miles of exposed ridge between the summits of Jefferson and Washington. The views into **Great Gulf** are spectacular. Then from Mount Washington, it is 4.5 miles down to the Cog Base Station area via Lakes of the Clouds and the Ammonoosuc Ravine Trail. Thus starting from Jefferson Notch, ascending the Ridge of Caps, traversing to Mt. Washington, and descending the Ammonoosuc Ravine provides an ambitious, 10.5-mile, high-mountain traverse.

Totals for the Mt. Jefferson to Mt. Washington traverse:
2–2½ hours, 3.6 miles, elevation gain: 1,350'

Trips from Lakes of the Clouds Hut

To Alpine Garden: In the alpine spring (late May, June), the grassy "lawns" on the east side of the mountain provide a fantastic display of color. Bigelow Lawn and the Alpine Garden are easily reached from the hut. Take Crawford Path and then **Tuckerman Crossover** through Tuckerman Junction on the Tuckerman Ravine Trail to **Alpine Garden Trail** at 1.2 miles. Walk left on the Alpine Garden Trail as far as you like, returning by the same route.

2–3 hours, 4–6 miles, elevation gain: about 1,000'

To Tuckerman Ravine: As above, proceed to Tuckerman Junction (1 mile) to pick up the Tuckerman Ravine Trail. Descend the headwall (very steep with loose rock in places) into the ravine to Hermit Lake Shelter. From here, it is 2.4 miles down to Pinkham Notch and NH 16.

3 hours, 4.6 miles, elevation gain: 500', loss: 3,500'

Maps: AMC: *#1 Presidential Range;* Map Adventures; Washburn: *Mt. Washington & The Heart of the Presidential Range;* Wilderness Maps: *Mt. Washington;* USGS: *Mt. Washington.*

Camping: There are two Forest Service campgrounds on Zealand Road and privately run campgrounds in Bartlett, Twin Mountain, Jefferson, Littleton, and Franconia. The AMC-run Crawford Notch Hostel provides rustic accommodations.

3 | Mount Adams and the Northern Presidentials

The great northern flank of the Presidentials seems to have an infinite number of trails, most of which ascend part or all the way up Mount Adams, the king of the northern peaks. The immense, upward sweep of the mountain, as seen from the highway, is one of the more impressive views in the White Mountains. Descriptions of the main hiking routes on Mounts Adams, Madison, and Jefferson follow. Many of the hikes originate from the parking area on US 2 known as **Appalachia**, 5.5 miles west of Gorham. Approaching from the south, take US 3 to Twin Mountain. Just north of Twin Mountain, follow NH 115 to Jefferson, and continue east on US 2 for 11 miles to Appalachia. The AMC's Hiker Shuttle services Appalachia. See the Great Gulf chapter for other approaches to the Northern Presidentials.

Mount Adams (5,774') via Valley Way

The views from Mt. Adams are among the best: Washington is 3.5 miles south, Jefferson is in the middle distance, and Madison is just a half mile to the northeast. The Carter Range is across the valley, and a vast forest stretches north toward Canada. Valley Way is the easiest route to **Madison Hut** (4,810'), and from the hut, both **Mt. Madison** (5,367') and Mt. Adams are readily climbed. Valley Way climbs steadily and directly with good footing, staying within earshot of a rushing brook much of the time, emerging from the woods just below the hut. From Madison Hut, the most direct route up Adams is via the Airline Trail. Follow **Gulfside Trail**, branching left onto **Air Line** after 15 minutes. Twenty more minutes will bring you to the top. Descend Valley Way or stay on the Air Line Trail (see below) to Appalachia, bypassing the hut.

7–8 hours, 9.6 miles, total climb: 4,500'

Approach: From Appalachia, on US 2, 5.5 miles west of Gorham.

Note: The Star Lake Trail (see map) is a fun and somewhat more difficult route up Adams. Follow signs from the hut.

Mount Madison from Gulfside Trail

Jared Gange

Mount Madison (5,367') via Watson Path

From Appalachia, start out on **Valley Way**, but at 2.4 miles (1½ hours), branch left on Watson Path. After crossing the brook, the trail climbs steeply over rough, rocky terrain. It is marked by cairns on the upper section. The views are great and improve steadily as you ascend the summit cone. From the top, descend the **Osgood Trail** (AT) in a westerly direction. (East will take you into Great Gulf, a different world.) About 20-30 minutes of easy rock scrambling brings you to the pleasures of Madison Hut, 550' below the summit. Valley Way (more direct, and protected from weather) is the preferred route back down to Appalachia. For those who are up for it, the 1,000'-climb up Mount Adams takes about 40 minutes from the hut (use Air Line). Doing both summits in a day is a popular but fairly demanding trip.

7 hours, 9.4 miles, total climb: 4,060' (Mt. Madison only)
Approach: Start and finish at Appalachia on US 2.

The Air Line up Mount Adams

Perhaps the classic route up Mount Adams, the Air Line ascends famous **Durand Ridge** and traverses the **Knife Edge**, high above King Ravine, before reaching the base of the upper slopes. From Appalachia, the Air Line branches (right) off **Valley Way** immediately. Several trail junctions are passed before the trail briefly merges with **Randolph Path**. Continuing, the trail gradually steepens as it ascends to the ridge crest. Soon after, the Scar Trail enters (left), views appear, and after passing Upper Bruin and Chemin des Dames (an escape route from King Ravine), the beautiful, open section of ridge known as the Knife Edge is finally reached. The trail then joins with the **Gulfside Trail** (AT) for a few minutes, before continuing to the top. Descend the same route or, for variety (and weather protection), take Valley Way.

> **8 hours, 8.6 miles, total climb: 4,500'**
>
> **Approach:** *Start from Appalachia, 5.5 miles west of Gorham.*

Star Lake and Mount Madison   Lars Gange

Randolph Path

Randolph Path climbs the north slopes of Mt. Adams in a traversing fashion, crossing or briefly coinciding with practically every major trail along the way before ending at **Edmands Col**, just north of Mount Jefferson. It is the old route—it was completed in 1899—from Randolph to Mount Jefferson. After crossing Sylvan Way, it intersects Valley Way (1.5 miles), and then Air Line before briefly teaming up with Short Line. Passing King Ravine, the route comes within a few minutes of the RMC's Log Cabin prior to crossing Lowe's Path into Cascade Ravine, passing close by another RMC facility, the Perch. Israel Ridge Path is joined briefly before the final, gentle swing over the top of Castle Ravine to Edmands Col, 0.6 mile from Jefferson's summit.

5 hours and 6 miles (ascent only). Elevation gain: 3,700'

Approach: From US 2, drive south on Dolly Copp Rd. (Pinkham B), 0.2 mile to the Randolph Path parking area.

King Ravine and Mount Adams

Perhaps the most difficult of the standard routes on Adams, King Ravine is full of large boulders, and we human creatures struggle over and around them as best we can. Starting from **Appalachia**, take **Air Line**, branching right onto **Randolph Path** at 0.9 mile. Climb gently along Randolph Path for 0.7 mile before taking **Short Line** (left) and ascending into the ravine, meeting **King Ravine Trail** at 2.6 miles from the car. The work begins here. Much of the time King Ravine Trail is just a paint-blazed route across big boulders, and since this deep ravine doesn't receive much sun, you may find the rocks slippery as well. (This is a very difficult trail for dogs.) Pockets of ice prevail long into summer. Note the RMC's Crag Camp high above on your right. **Chemin des Dames** provides an escape—it exits left, climbing very steeply to the Airline Trail. At the top of the headwall—a tough 1,200' climb—King Ravine Trail ends on the Air Line. Continue on this to the summit. Descend on Airline or Valley Way, with an optional visit to Madison Hut.

9 hours, 9 miles, elevation gain: 4,550'

Approach: From Appalachia, 5.5 miles west of Gorham on US 2.

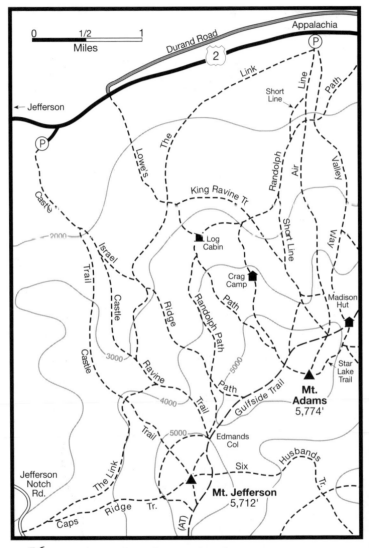

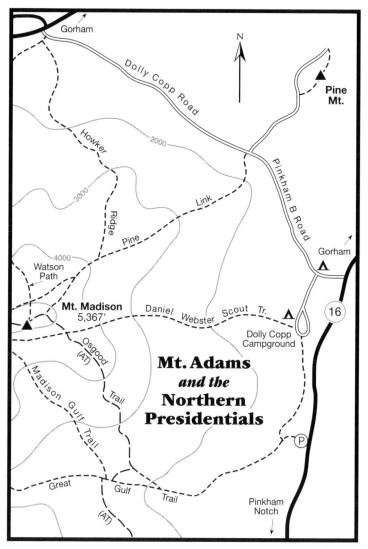

Randolph Mountain Club

The Randolph Mountain Club has maintained hiking trails in the Northern Presidential area since 1910. The club's guide book, *Randolph Paths*, provides a good introduction to the trails and attractions of the area. High on the north flank of Adams, the RMC has two fine cabins, Gray Knob at 4,400' (next to Lowe's Path) and nearby Crag Camp (4,250'), perched dramatically on the edge of King Ravine. Caretakers are in residence all year; overnight guests pay a small fee. Space is available on a first come, first serve basis. The Perch (4,300') is a shelter and tent platform located on Perch Path, just west of Randolph Path and 1.1 miles below Edmands Col. The Log Cabin (uninsulated and with an open doorway), is on Lowe's Path at 3,250'. For more information, write to the RMC in Randolph, NH 03570.

Lowe's Path

Even older than Randolph Path, Lowe's Path (completed in 1876) sees much less use today than 50 or 100 years ago. From Lowe's Store, it starts across US 2 (and a little to the west), ascending Mount Adams at a pleasant and generally even gradient. Lowe's Path is considered the easiest route up Mount Adams, and it reaches the summit after 4.8 miles. After crossing the Link, you reach the RMC's **Log Cabin**, about halfway both in time and distance. About 45 minutes later, pass the short spur trail (left) to **Gray Knob** (RMC cabin). Now ascend the northwest ridge of Adams, contouring slightly below Sam Adams (5,585') to reach the high col known as **Thunderstorm Junction**. From here, make the 500' climb to the summit and the all-encompassing views: Mt. Jefferson and Mt. Madison are on either side, and to the south, Mt. Washington rises out of the depths of Great Gulf. The Carter Range and the Mahoosucs are in full view. Descend the way you came up.

8 hours, 9.6 miles, elevation: 4,400'

Approach: The trailhead is across US 2 from Lowe's Store, two miles west of Appalachia and 7.5 miles west of Gorham. Park at the store (small fee).

Mount Jefferson (5,712') via Castle Ravine and Castellated Ridge

This is a very interesting, but somewhat arduous route up Mount Jefferson. Take the **Castle Trail** for 1.7 miles over easy terrain to the **Israel Ridge Trail**, with several stream crossings along the way. Branch left, continuing for 0.4 mile before heading right on the **Castle Ravine Trail**. After crossing and recrossing the brook—at times the trail is in the brook—reach the base of the headwall. Continue climbing, out in the open now, carefully following blazes and cairns up the steep, and at times loose, rocks. It is very easy to stray off route! Be sure you have plenty to drink—on a hot day, the upper ravine can feel like a desert. Once on the ridge, bear right on **Randolph Path** a short distance to **Edmands Col** and Gulfside Trail, before following **Jefferson Loop** to the summit, at about 5.5 miles. The 4.8-mile descent is entirely on the Castle Trail. It starts from the large cairn, just east of the summit, and runs along the prominent northwest ridge: Castellated Ridge. A beautiful route with dramatic views into the ravine, it is also exposed to weather for nearly 1.5 miles. After negotiating the "castles" (rock outcrops which will involve some scrambling) the trail drops steeply through woods. And after passing Israel Ridge Path (right), the gradient eases for the final stroll back to the car.

8 hours, 10.3 miles, elevation gain: 4,220'
Approach: *Park just off US 2 at Bowman, 4.3 miles east of Jefferson (NH 115), or a mile west of Lowe's Store.*

The Link

The Link, a lower elevation version of Randolph Path, connects **Jefferson Notch** (branches left from Caps Ridge Trail) with Appalachia. Contouring the west side of Jefferson, it climbs gently (but with rough footing) to cross **Castellated Ridge** before dropping steeply into Castle Ravine. Descending, it merges briefly with Israel Ridge, dips into Cascade Ravine, and intersects Lowe's Path at about 2,500'. Swinging across the base of Mount Adams, it joins the Amphibrach to end at **Appalachia**. The total length of the Link is 7.5 miles.

Lakes of the Clouds Hut to Madison Hut

A classic section of the Appalachian Trail, this 7-mile alpine traverse is the highest and most exposed route in the White Mountains. From Lakes of the Clouds, ascend Mount Washington on **Crawford Path** (1.5 miles), and continue northward on the **Gulfside Trail**, soon crossing the top of Great Gulf's impressive headwall. At 2.9 miles, Mt. Clay is reached (Clay Loop passes over the summit) and at 4.7 miles, Mount Jefferson. The Gulfside Trail stays below and east of the summit, but the extra effort over the top via Jefferson Loop is well worth it. Beyond Edmands Col, the Gulfside Trail leads to Thunderstorm Junction. Here, a short detour—a 500' climb—takes you to the top of Mt. Adams. Continuing, the Gulfside Trail descends to Madison Hut at 4,810'.

> *5–6 hours, 7 miles, elevation gain: 2,585'*
> *Bad weather variation: Descend east into Great Gulf on the Sphinx Trail (at the col between Jefferson and Clay), or take Randolph Path from Edmands Col toward Gray Knob Cabin, on the northwest slope.*

Howker Ridge, Mount Madison

Howker Ridge is the northeast ridge of Mt. Madison. Start on Randolph Path, immediately branching left on the **Howker Ridge Trail**. Climb through woods, passing interesting streams and waterfalls along the way. Only after about 2 to 2½ hours of hiking, and after crossing the second howk, do the really good views appear. There are nice, open views from the third and especially from the final howk at 4,300'. In about another half mile, you reach the **Osgood Trail**. Head right on it for 0.2 mile to the summit and its panoramic views. Descend (west) to **Madison Hut**. Take Valley Way down to Appalachia. From here it is only 0.9 mile back to the Howker Ridge trailhead along US 2 and Dolly Copp Road.

> *7 hours, 8.7 miles (and 0.9 mile on road), elev. gain: 4,120'*
> *Approach: From the Randolph Path trailhead on Dolly Copp Road, 0.2 mile south of US 2.*

Maps: RMC: *Randolph Valley and the No. Peaks of the Pres. Range*; AMC: *#1 Pres. Range*; DeLorme; Map Adventures; Washburn: *Mt. Washington*.

Mountain Weather

Mountain weather, particularly on mountains that extend above treeline, poses a risk to the hiker. This is due to the fact that in terms of climate, as you gain altitude, you travel north. The upper slopes of the Presidentials have the climate of northern Labrador. The lack of trees or other natural protection exposes you to the full force of the wind. Thus on the higher New England peaks, hikers and other mountain visitors, after a few hours effort, typically find themselves in arctic or sub-arctic environments, where severe storms can occur any day of the year.

Of course the weather can be pleasant, and a fair amount of the time it is, although good conditions may last for only an hour or two! But even on "good" days, lower temperatures and cooler breezes are the rule. Regardless of forecast and temperature when starting out, be prepared for worse weather. High winds and driving rain will quickly wear down even strong hikers. If the weather is bad, or clearly deteriorating, do not hesitate to turn back!

The above discussion applies with double emphasis to Mount Washington. Because it is the highest mountain in the area—it is the dominant physical feature of New England—storms hit Mount Washington with unusual force. If that were not enough, three major storm tracks converge in the area. During the hurricane of 1934, the wind at the summit measured 231 mph, the world record. Winds reach hurricane force (75 mph) about 100 days out of the year. While it is probably not the case that Mount Washington has the worst weather in the world—Antarctica and Mt. Everest come to mind—its great accessibility and high winds combine to make it possibly the most *dangerous* small mountain in the world.

Camping: *Dolly Copp (on NH 16), Moose Brook State Park (Gorham) and private campgrounds in Jefferson, Berlin, and Shelburne.*

4 Gorham–Randolph Area

The nine hikes in this chapter start from or near US 2 in the Gorham–Randolph–Jefferson area. Lookout Ledge, Mascot Pond, Pine Mountain, Mount Evans, and Mount Crag are great hikes for families with young children. They offer excellent views of the nearby Presidential Range, the river valleys, and the less-travelled woods to the north. The Randolph Mountain Club's *Randolph Paths* (see references) provides a detailed guide to the trails in the area. Two 4,000-footers, Cabot and Waumbek, are included in this chapter.

Mount Cabot 4,170'

The appeal of Cabot, the most northerly of the 4,000-footers, is enhanced by a cabin (owned by the Forest Service and maintained by local Boy Scouts) located near the summit. The cabin is available for use winter and summer on a first-come, first-serve basis. From its trailhead, follow the **York Pond Trail** (here a gravel-road) just 0.2 mile before branching right onto the **Bunnell Notch Trail**. Follow this over moderate (in places wet) terrain, reaching **Kilkenny Ridge Trail** at 3 miles from your car. Head north (right) on Kilkenny Ridge Trail (at second intersection, first heads south). You soon join with the **Mt. Cabot Trail** (enters left). After 1.7 miles from Kilkenny Ridge Trail, and over a thousand feet of climbing, you reach Cabot's summit. Return the way you came. Cabot can also be climbed from the north via Unknown Pond and the Horn (3,905'). See Chapter 6.

> *6 hours, 9.4 miles, total climb: 2,600'*
>
> ***Approach:*** *From NH 110, take York Pond Road (F.R. 13) to York Pond. Continue past the gate by the fish hatchery for 2.1 miles to the gated (signed) trailhead on the left.*

The **Kilkenny Ridge Trail** offers a good 2–3 day backpack. It runs from South Pond (just off NH 110) south past Unknown Pond and over the Horn to Mt. Cabot. From Cabot it continues in a southerly direction, crossing Mt. Weeks (3,890') and finally ending on the summit of Mt. Waumbek (4,006'), a total distance of about 21 miles.

Mt. Waumbek and Mt. Starr King (3,915')

Although Mount Starr King is the "star" of this hike because it has the better view, slightly higher Mount Waumbek, at 4,006' and a mile farther on, is the final destination for many hikers. From the parking area at the top of the driveway head up old logging roads, staying on the main route. The trail climbs steadily and uneventfully, working around to the west before reaching the summit from the north. The good viewpoint is about 200' beyond, at a former shelter site. From here, the trail to Mount Waumbek continues along the adjoining ridge, reaching the wooded summit and the **Kilkenny Ridge Trail** after a mile. Return by the same route.

5½ hours, 7.2 miles, total climb: 2,600'
4 hours and 5.2 miles for Mt. Starr King only
Approach: From Jefferson, drive east on US 2 for 0.2 mile, then turn left up the driveway opposite the golf course sign.

Owl's Head 3,258'

Owl's Head is the north spur of **Cherry Mountain**. Its graceful, symmetrical cone shape is easy to pick out from Jefferson. The open ledges of Owl's Head offer stunning views—among the very best!—of Washington, Jefferson and Adams, about 10 miles to the east. From the road the trail circles through a flat area, crosses a brook at 1.1 miles, then climbs steadily up the mountain, before making the final push up a northwest ridge to the top. Use care following the trail through logged areas. Return the same way. In 1885, a huge landslide on the west side of Owl's Head launched about a million tons of debris into the valley below.

3.5 hours, 5 miles, total climb: 2,000'
Approach: The trailhead is on NH 115, 3.9 miles south of US 2 in Jefferson. Or, from Twin Mountain on US 302, drive north for 7.7 miles, first on US 3, then right on NH 115.

Note: Mount Martha (3,573') is the highest point of Cherry Mountain. An 0.8-mile trail called **Martha's Mile** links Owl's Head with the summit, where some viewpoints have been cut.

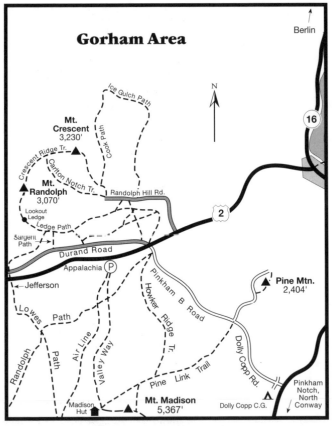

Lookout Ledge 2,350'

Considered to be one of the better of the lower viewpoints in the area, Lookout Ledge is easily reached by the 1.3-mile **Ledge Trail**. Views of the almost mile-high wall of the Northern Presidentials and of the Carter Range reward hikers. The ledge can also be reached by the shorter (0.8 mile) and steeper

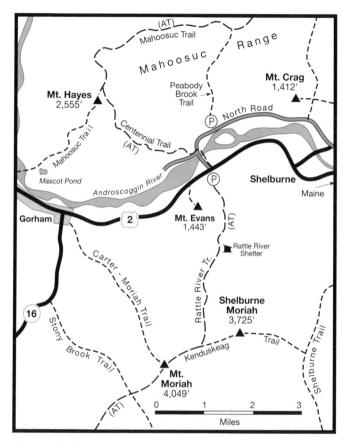

Sargent Path, which starts from Durand Road, 0.8 mile to the west of Ravine House Site.

   2 hours, 2.6 miles, total climb: 930'

   Approach: *Drive to Ravine House Site, 0.9 mile west on Durand Rd. from the US 2 access east of Appalachia.*

Ice Gulch

This challenging hike does not lead to a summit, nor are there any noteworthy viewpoints along the way, but the boulder-choked ravine is definitely worth a visit. Ice lingers well into the summer in the more protected crevices. Take **Cook Path** (it branches off **Mount Crescent Trail** after 0.1 mile) as it ascends across the east flank of Mt. Crescent, reaching the top of Ice Gulch at 2.6 miles. Descend the rocky labyrinth of Ice Gulch, negotiating various awkward and difficult spots. Eventually the trail turns right and works its way across easy ground, returning to Randolph Hill Road about 0.6 mile below your starting point.

3½ hours, 6.6 miles, total climb: 1,000'

Approach: 3.5 miles west of Gorham turn right on Randolph Hill Road. Mt. Crescent Trail is at the end of the public road. The trails are well marked by the Randolph Mountain Club.

Pine Mountain 2,404'

Lying in the shadow of the 4,000'-high north flank of Mount Madison, Pine Mountain offers perhaps the best view of all the lower vantage points in this area. The view east to the Carter Range is especially fine. From Pinkham B Road (also called Dolly Copp Rd.), follow the private (gated) Pine Mountain Road on your right for 0.8 mile over easy, rolling terrain to Pine Mountain proper. Here the **Ledge Trail** branches right and climbs the remaining 600' to the summit and great views. Return by the same route.

2 hours, 3 miles, total climb: 800'

Approach: From Dolly Copp Campground (on NH 16), drive 2 miles on Pinkham B Road to Pine Mountain Road.

Mascot Pond

Cross the Androscoggin River on a pedestrian walkway, which hangs under the railroad bridge, and head right along a dirt road (no blazes) for about a half mile to a small power station. Cross the dam by walking between the two buildings. Walk left up the road about 100 yards to the **Mahoosuc Trail** on the right (sign). The wide, pleasant trail (blue blazes) climbs steadily, at times paralleling a rushing stream. After about ¾ mile, at a "Y", bear right on the well-used path to the pond. The attractive, south-facing beach is a great swimming and picnicking spot. Return the same way.

1½ hours, 2.6 miles, total climb: 360'

Approach: *Start at the RR bridge on NH 16, just north of the US 2/NH 16 intersection on the west side of Gorham.*

Mount Evans 1,443'

Mount Evans offers a short but fairly steep climb to good views of the Androscoggin River Valley and the Mahoosucs, across the river. From the highway, walk straight up the hill—stay left of the house—to a small clearing. Bear right through the clearing onto a rough and wet logging road—after about 100 yards, the yellow-blazed trail bears left; you should see a sign. Climbing through dense woods, it soon gains a small ridge before switchbacking up to the top. Blueberry bushes and heather grow on Mount Evans' open summit.

1 hour, 1.4 miles, total climb: 650'

Approach: *From Gorham, drive 2.7 miles east on US 2 to a driveway (sign) on the right. Park on the shoulder of US 2.*

Mount Crag 1,412'

A hike with about as much climbing as Mount Evans (above), Mount Crag offers good views up and down the Androscoggin River and of the much higher Carter Range across the valley. Walk through the little turnstyle gate and follow **Austin Brook Trail** (a woods road) for 0.4 mile to where it crosses the **Yellow Trail**. Head left here and make the enjoyable 0.8-mile climb through an open mixed forest to the clifftop summit.

1½ hours, 2.4 miles, total climb: 680'

Approach: *From Shelburne (east of Gorham, on US 2), head left on Meadow Road, then left on North Road for 0.6 mile.*

Maps: RMC; DeLorme; USGS: *Berlin, Carter Dome, Shelburne, Pliny Range.*

Campgrounds: *In Carroll, Jefferson, Shelburne and Moose Brook S.P.*

5 Mahoosuc Range

North of the Presidential Range, and just east of Gorham, the Appalachian Trail crosses US 2 and begins its traverse of the rugged Mahoosuc Range. The passage through the jumbled boulders of Mahoosuc Notch is considered the most difficult on the entire Appalachian Trail. The range never rises above treeline, but open ledges provide ample views. There are excellent day hikes here, to alpine ponds and rocky summits. Success Pond Road, a heavily used logging road that starts in Berlin and parallels the range on the west, provides the access for most of these shorter excursions. The high point of the range is Old Speck Mountain (4,180'), just over the border in Maine, above Grafton Notch. The Mahoosucs are not part of the White Mountain National Forest, and at lower elevations the land is very actively logged, primarily to produce pulp for paper. Success Pond Road is a private road and is subject to closure or re-routing without notice.

Mount Success 3,565'

Mount Success has great views of the Presidentials from the open areas to the south of its summit. Take the **Success Trail**, entering the forest at 0.5 mile (sign) after following a woods road. Climb steadily; in about a mile you'll see a spur trail to the right. Take it a quarter mile in for the superb view of the Presidentials. Head back to the trail and ascend to the ridge. When you reach the **Mahoosuc Trail** (MT), follow it 0.6 mile (right) through woods to the summit. There's a view of the Carter Range and the Presidentials, and the Vermont mountains are visible to the west. Return by the same route.

4 hours, 6 miles, total climb: 2,020'

Approach: The trailhead is located 5.4 miles up Success Pond Road from Berlin, on the right.

Mount Carlo (3,565') and Goose Eye (3,860')

Begin your exploration of the Mahoosucs with this one! The views from Goose Eye and Carlo are superb. The first mile from

Speck Pond in winter   Matthew Cull

Success Pond Road is easy woods walking. The trail then steepens, ascends a ravine, and reaches **Carlo Col Shelter** at 2.4 miles. Climb another 0.3 mile to **Carlo Col** and the **Mahoosuc Trail**. Now head north (left) on the MT (also the AT) for 0.4 mile of climbing to reach the broad, open summit of Carlo. North of the summit, the trail descends over interesting terrain—with spectacular views—into another col, only to climb again, at times very briskly, reaching **Goose Eye Trail** 1.4 miles from Carlo's summit. Head left 0.1 mile to the open summit of impressive Goose Eye Mountain for the high point of the trip. After relaxing a bit, continue (west) on the Goose Eye Trail, first negotiating a very small cliff (there's a rope—this is not difficult) just below the summit. From here, the trail glides down into woods, eventually crossing a brook before following a woods road for the final mile back to the car and the completion of the loop.

5 hours, 7.5 miles, total climb: 2,575'

Approach: *From Berlin, drive out Success Pond Road 8 miles. The Carlo Col trailhead is on the right.*

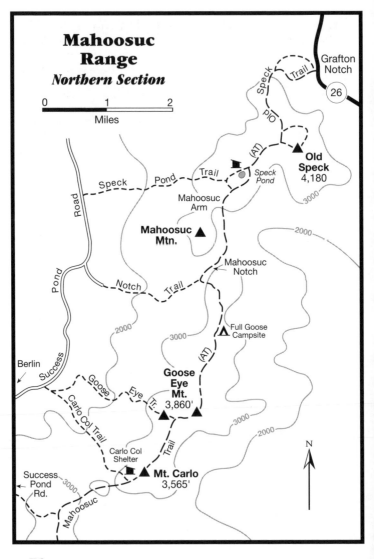

Mahoosuc Range
Northern Section

0   1   2
Miles

Grafton Notch

Trail 1

Speck

P10

26

(AT)

Speck Pond Trail

Speck Pond

Old Speck
4,180

3000

Road

Mahoosuc Arm

Mahoosuc Mtn.

2000

Mahoosuc Notch

Pond

Notch Trail

2000

3000

Full Goose Campsite

(AT)

Berlin

Success

Goose Eye Tr.

Goose Eye Mt.
3,860'

3000

2000

Carlo Col Trail

Trail

N

Carlo Col Shelter

Mt. Carlo
3,565'

Success Pond Rd.

3000

Mahoosuc

Mahoosuc Notch and Speck Pond (3,430')

A very long day hike, the trip to Speck Pond is probably more enjoyable as an overnight trip. From the road take **Notch Trail** along logging roads and through wet areas for 2.2 miles to the Mahoosuc Trail, then left to reach the top of dreaded Mahoosuc Notch! The next mile presents a difficult struggle with awkward-sized boulders. Exit left and climb moderately, then steeply, on the tough, winding trail up **Mahoosuc Arm** (3,777'). After crossing its broad, somewhat open summit, the MT wastes no time descending to Speck Pond. Speck Pond Campsite (summer caretaker) is at the north end of the pond. Return by the same route or via **Speck Pond Trail** (4.5 mi. to Success Pond Rd.), avoiding the Notch.

8-10 hours, 11.6 miles, total climb: 3,280'

Approach: From Berlin drive 11 miles north on Success Pond Road to the side road (right) which ends at the trailhead.

Old Speck (4,180') from Grafton Notch

Old Speck is Maine's third highest mountain, and from its summit tower there are wide views. From the parking area in spectacular Grafton Notch, follow the **Old Speck Trail** (the AT south). After passing the Eyebrow Trail (a loop trail) at 0.1 mile, climb switchbacks up past the falls of Cascade Brook, and meet the upper junction of the Eyebrow Trail at 1.1 miles. At about 3.5 miles leave the AT and branch left on the **Mahoosuc Trail** for 0.3 mile to the summit. The tower (in poor repair) lifts you above the trees for views of Sunday River Ski Area, the Mahoosucs and, farther to the south, Mount Adams and the Presidentials. Descend by the same route.

5½ hours, 7.6 miles, total climb: 2,700'

Approach: From Bethel, Maine (east of Gorham on US 2), drive north on Maine Route 26 to Grafton Notch.

Traverse of the Mahoosuc Range

Although its wilderness character is compromised by intensive logging on the west and a major ski area on the east, the 32-mile traverse of the Mahoosucs is a classic backcountry excursion. Access to the interior sections of the range is somewhat inconvenient and, although the Appalachian Trail traverses it, there are far fewer hikers here than in the Presidentials just to the south. We present it as a four–day trip, although five or six days is common.

Day 1 Gorham to Trident Col: From Route 16 cross the river on the RR bridge walkway and head right on an unmarked road for a half mile; cross the canal and find the blue-blazed **Mahoosuc Trail**. Climb moderately, passing the Mascot Pond spur trail at 1.1 miles, and cresting **Mt. Hayes** (views) at 3.1 miles and **Cascade Mtn.** (open summit) at 5.1 miles. After a steep descent, Trident Col is reached at 6.5 miles, where a spur trail leads left to tent sites.

Day 2 Trident Col to Carlo Col Shelter: After passing Page Pond (one mile) the trail climbs to a good viewpoint on the side of Bald Cap. Continuing over mixed terrain, the MT reaches **Dream Lake** about 2.5 miles from Trident Col. Here the Peabody Brook Trail departs right. Popular **Gentian Pond** (tent sites and a shelter) is 2.2 miles farther along. From the pond, the climb up **Mt. Success** is interesting (steep at times) with great views near the top. It's 2.5 miles on to **Carlo Col** and **Carlo Col Trail**—head left 0.3 mile to the fine Carlo Col Shelter—making it 10 miles total for day two.

Day 3 Carlo Col to Full Goose Shelter: The broad, open summit of **Mt. Carlo** is just 0.4 mile north of Carlo Col. Then descend across open ledges and make the steep climb up spectacular **Goose Eye Mtn.** (1.8 miles from Carlo Col). Continue along the interesting ridge, crossing from East Peak to North Peak of Goose Eye. From here it is a mile down to Full Goose Shelter, which is perched on a ledge. This makes for a short day: about 5 miles.

Day 4 Full Goose Shelter to Old Speck and Grafton Notch: From the shelter, hike the half mile to the South Peak of **Fulling Mill Mountain** and continue to the top of **Mahoosuc Notch** at 1.5 miles. Descend into the confines of the Notch with care: this is a difficult, awkward mile! Then make the arduous but interesting climb out of the notch and across **Mahoosuc Arm**, before dropping down to **Speck Pond**, where there is a tenting area. **Old Speck Mtn.** (at 4,180 the trip high point) is 1.4 miles farther. From here, the Old Speck Trail and the AT bring you down to Grafton Notch (on ME 26), concluding your traverse. Mileage for the fourth day is 10.3.

Total distance: 32 miles, total climb: about 10,000'

Maps: AMC: #6 North Country - Mahoosucs; USGS: Pliny Range, Berlin.

Campgrounds: Gorham (Moose Brook S. P.), Berlin, and Shelburne.

Appalachian Trail in the Mahoosucs

Richard Bailey

The Appalachian Trail

The 2,100-mile Appalachian Trail is the premier long-distance hiking path in the U.S. Starting in Georgia, the "AT" runs along the crest of the Smokies, Virginia's Blue Ridge Mountains, Massachusetts' Berkshires, Vermont's Green Mountains, and the White Mountains of New Hampshire before traversing many miles of Maine wilderness to end on the summit of Mount Katahdin, Maine's highest peak. Of the 2,000 hikers starting out each spring from Georgia, hoping to reach Maine before the onset of winter, only about 200 complete the trip. Most hikers take a section by section approach and visit the trail over a period of years. The AT enters New Hampshire mid-state in Hanover and traverses most of the highest mountains: Moosilauke, the Kinsmans, Lafayette, the Garfield and Twin Ranges, Mt. Washington and the entire Presidential Range, and the Carter Range before finishing with the less-travelled Mahoosuc Range. The AMC's system of eight huts, placed on or near the trail from Franconia Notch to Carter Notch, provides a unique opportunity for hut-to-hut hiking.

Mount Hayes 2,555'

A visit to lovely **Mascot Pond**, cliffs overlooking Gorham, and an open, rocky summit are some of the attractions of this hike. This is also the initial section of the 32-mile traverse of the entire Mahoosuc Range. After crossing the river on the pedestrian footbridge, follow the gravel road right, soon crossing a canal. Follow the blue blazes marking the Mahoosuc Trail. After some climbing, at times along a brook, come to the side trail (right, 0.3 mile) to Mascot Pond, a little over a mile from NH 16. The pond's sandy beach is a great spot for a picnic and a swim. The open, flattish summit of Mount Hayes is two miles farther along on the Mahoosuc Trail, and its best views are obtained by following the short spur trail to the right. Return by the same route.

4 hours, 6.2 miles, total climb: 1,740'

Approach: Start at the RR bridge on NH 16, just north of the US 2/NH 16 intersection on the west side of Gorham.

Note: The hike to Mascot Pond is a local favorite. See Chapter 4 for a detailed description.

Dream Lake and the Peabody Brook Trail

Although the Mahoosuc Trail (MT) officially begins in Gorham from NH 16, the Peabody Brook Trail or the Centennial Trail (AT) are more popular ways to begin the Mahoosuc traverse. Peabody Brook Trail runs from North Road to Dream Lake and continues another 0.1 mile to the Mahoosuc Trail. For its first mile or so, the trail is along a logging road. It gets fairly steep in its middle portion (there is a ladder at one point), but the grade eases on the final section. Those wanting a longer hike can continue right at the MT intersection for two miles to pretty **Gentian Pond**. In any event, return the way you came. Accessing the MT by the Peabody Brook Trail reduces the total Mahoosuc traverse by six miles.

4 hours, 6.2 miles, total climbing: 1,900'

Approach: From US 2, 3.3 miles east of Gorham, head left across the river, then right 1.3 miles to the trailhead.

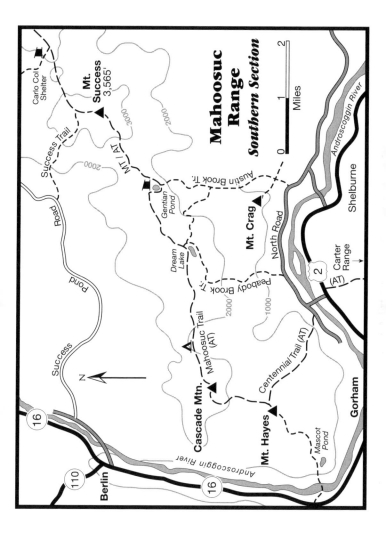

Mahoosuc Range

Southern Section

Mt. Success 3,565'

Carlo Col Shelter

Success Trail

Road

Pond

Success

MT / AT

Gentian Pond

Dream Lake

Austin Brook Tr.

Mt. Crag

North Road

Peabody Brook Tr.

2000

1000

2000

Mahoosuc Trail (AT)

Cascade Mtn.

Centennial Trail (AT)

Mt. Hayes

Mascot Pond

Androscoggin River

Berlin

Gorham

Shelburne

Carter Range

Androscoggin River

2

16

110

N

Miles

0 1 2

6 The North Country

The northernmost part of the state—generally the land north of NH 110 and Route 2—is referred to as "the North Country." Forest is king here, and this is logging country. The mountains are lower with fewer hiking trails, and the recreation tends to be of the hunting and fishing variety. In winter snowmobiles cruise the hundreds of miles of logging roads. There is excellent hiking near Stark and Dixville Notch, as well as farther to the north. Percy Peak and Unknown Pond are two very worthwhile trips in the southern part of this region.

Mount Forist 2,068'

Mount Forist's granite cliff rises majestically above the city of Berlin, like something out of Yosemite. Keep left of the house at the end of Madigan St. and follow the unmarked, indistinct trail—at times almost straight up—among boulders, birches and blueberries. When the grade eases, bear right across the clifftop (in dense woods) to various viewpoints. Berlin and its smokestacks are directly below with the Mahoosucs in the distance.

1½ hours roundtrip, total climb: 700'
Approach: *In Berlin, follow NH 110 to Madigan Street, turn left and drive uphill to the end. This is about 0.5 mile from Dunkin Donuts.*

Devil's Slide 1,700'

Devil's Slide is the name given to the impressive 700' cliff in the little settlement of Stark. A very steep trail up the west side of the mountain leads to some dramatic ledges, with views of the covered bridge directly below and Mount Cabot to the south. From your car, walk to the top of the field and enter the woods. Bear left at the cabin and follow the trail, variously marked with pink and orange tape and blazes, to the top. The trail is extremely steep near the top. The actual summit is wooded with very limited views.

1 hour roundtrip, 1.5 miles, total climb: 700'
Approach: *Stark is on NH 110, a few miles east of Groveton. Cross the covered bridge and bear left. Park after 0.7 miles.*

Unknown Pond and the Horn   Jared Gange

Unknown Pond and the Horn

Nestled in a vast forest, Unknown Pond is a beautiful spot. From the gate on Forest Road #11, walk down the road about 0.8 mile to where **Unknown Pond Trail** (sign) branches left and begins its moderate and steady climb to Unknown Pond. Most of the trail is in a birch woods. Once at the pond, there is an excellent view of the Horn (3,905'), a pointed summit 1.7 miles to the south. Take **Kilkenny Ridge Trail**, and then a side trail (left), to the Horn's ledgy summit for good views of the surrounding area. **Mount Cabot**, at 4,170', lies a further 1.1 miles south on the Kilkenny Ridge Trail. (The normal approach to Cabot is described in Chapter 4.) Unknown Pond can also be reached on the Kilkenny Ridge Trail from South Pond (6.8 miles) via **Rogers Ledge**.

4 hours, 6 miles, total climb: 1,450'
To the Horn: roundtrip is 9.5 miles and total climb: 2,250'
Approach: Just east of Stark village (on NH 110) follow Mill Brook Road (Forest Road #11) south 3.7 miles south to the gate and park.

Rogers Ledge 2,965'

From the trailhead (signs for Devil's Hopyard) at South Pond Recreation Area, head south on the **Kilkenny Ridge Trail**. At 0.7 mile the trail to Devil's Hopyard branches right. From here it is 3.4 miles to the top of Roger's Ledge, the highest point on the ridge of Deer Mountain. Travelling over generally moderate terrain, the trail does steepen considerably in the last half mile. The side trail right, just before the summit, leads to the views from the cliff's edge—across the forest of the Kilkenny region towards Cabot and the Horn, the Mahoosucs, and the Presidentials.

5 hours and 8.2 miles roundtrip. Elevation gain: 2,000'

Approach: From NH 110, between Stark and West Milan, turn south (well-signed) to the South Pond Recreation Area.

North Percy 3,418'

This is a great hike and popular with the locals: it's known for good blueberries in season. The trail ascends a variety of terrain before reaching the open summit. For the first mile it climbs moderately, with Slide Brook just below you. It then gets quite steep as it moves onto bare rock, before veering sharply right to traverse some low-angle slabs. The trail soon threads its way along a curious little rock rib to reach the col between North and South Percy. Bear left and continue through very dense woods soon coming out onto the fun, granite slabs which lead to the summit. The broad top has views in all directions. Descend the same route. North Percy is the most interesting mountain in the area, and there are impressive views of it from Route 110. The bushwhack trail to the summit of **South Percy** has been blazed and wided: the steep ledges of South Percy add more great views to this hike. The **Cohos Trail** traverses the Percy Peaks from southeast to northwest.

3½ hours, 4.4 miles, total climb: 2,140'

Approach: Drive east 2.5 miles on NH 110 from Groveton and head left on Emerson Road. Cross the river, bear right, then sharply left (second left) onto Nash Stream Road. Follow it for 2.7 miles to the trailhead (sign) on the right, just past Slide Brook.

North Percy Peak from South Percy Richard Bailey

Sugarloaf Mountain 3,701'

The trail to Sugarloaf is located 5.5 miles north of the Percy trail-head. Its open summit offers excellent views of the area, especially of North Percy, only five miles away. From the parking area walk left of the camp and continue into the woods, following an old service road for about an hour as it climbs steadily to two abandoned cabins. From here it is about a half mile to the top. The trail bears right, approaching the summit from the north. On clear days the Presidentials are visible, far to the south.

3½ hours, 4.2 miles, total climb: 2,170'

Approach: As for North Percy above, take Emerson Road to Nash Stream Road. See the map. Continue for 8.2 miles to trailhead parking on the left.

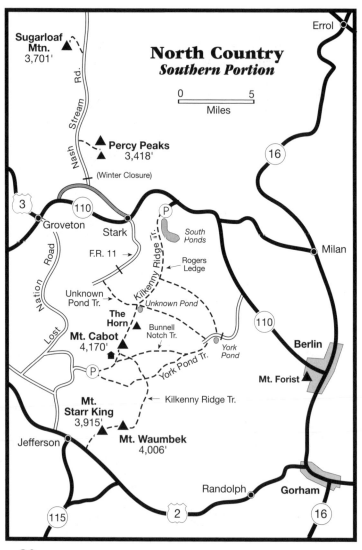

North Country
Southern Portion

0   5

Miles

Errol

16

Sugarloaf Mtn.
3,701'

Nash Stream Rd.

Percy Peaks
3,418'

(Winter Closure)

3

110

Groveton

Stark

P

South Ponds

Milan

F.R. 11 →

Rogers Ledge

Kilkenny Ridge Tr.

Unknown Pond Tr.

Unknown Pond

The Horn

Mt. Cabot
4,170'

Bunnell Notch Tr.

110

York Pond

Berlin

P

York Pond Tr.

Mt. Forist

← Kilkenny Ridge Tr.

Mt. Starr King
3,915'

Mt. Waumbek
4,006'

Jefferson

Randolph

Gorham

115

2

16

Nation Road

Lost

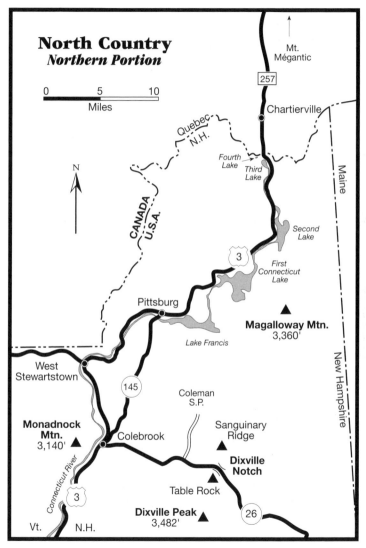

North Country
Northern Portion

0   5   10
Miles

N

Mt. Mégantic

257

Chartierville

Quebec
N.H.

CANADA
U.S.A.

Fourth
Lake

Third
Lake

Second
Lake

3

First
Connecticut
Lake

Maine

Pittsburg

▲ Magalloway Mtn.
3,360'

Lake Francis

New Hampshire

West
Stewartstown

145

Coleman
S.P.

Monadnock
Mtn. ▲
3,140'

Colebrook

Sanguinary
Ridge ▲

Dixville
Notch

3

Table Rock ▲

26

Connecticut River

Dixville Peak ▲
3,482'

Vt.   N.H.

Dixville Notch

Dixville Notch is on Highway 26 between Colebrook (12 miles to the west) and Errol. The eastern approach is through a vast spruce and balsam forest while the notch itself is surprisingly narrow, with steep cliffs on either side. Occupying the land just west of the notch proper, along the shores of Lake Gloriette, is the large **Balsams Grand Resort Hotel**, a full-service resort well off the beaten path. The hotel maintains a small alpine ski area, cross country skiing and hiking trails for its guests and the public. The resort produces an excellent map of the various hiking trails. About a mile east of the resort, at the Dixville Notch State Wayside, there are picnic facilities and several interesting flumes.

Dixville Peak 3,482'

The cleared summit of Dixville Peak—the highest mountain in the area—offers good views of the North Country. To the west, you see into Vermont, and to the north, across Dixville Notch towards the Connecticut Lakes. Up until now, most of the visitors to the summit have arrived on a snowmobile; with the creation of the **Cohos Trail** perhaps hikers will make up a larger share. The shortest route to the top is to take XC ski trail #11 (starts at the base of the alpine ski area) and then continue on the (rather steep) snowmobile trail to the summit. Alternatively, one can follow the Cohos Trail: Take Balsams Resort hiking trail D2 to Table Rock (photo page 83), continue past the top of the ski area (on trail D3) pick up trail J which leads to the above snowmobile trail (head left) for the final climb.

> ***3 hours and 5 miles. Elevation gain: 1,700' (short route)***
> ***Approach:*** *From the Balsams Resort's ski area (short route) or the trailhead on NH 26, near the resort's east entrance. See the Balsam Resort map.*

Maps: The Balsams: *Trail Map & Guide*; AMC: *#6 North Country-Mahoosucs*; USGS: *Sherbrooke, Groveton, Percy Peaks*; Topaz Maps: *New Hampshire Outdoor Recreation Map;* Delorme: *NH Atlas & Gazetteer*

Table Rock   Ed Rolfe

Table Rock 2,540'

Towering over the highway south of Balsams Resort, Table Rock catches the eye. Offering a short hike with a spectacular finish, it is the jagged shoulder of **Mount Gloriette** (2,780'). The final section crosses a very narrow ridge, with a sheer drop-off on either side, and will not appeal to everyone. From the parking area, take XC trail #5, but immediately branch left onto the trail proper (hiking trail D1) and ascend easy grades for about 0.7 mile to a junction. The short, exposed spur trail leads left to the dramatic viewpoint. Use the same trail for the descent, or continue east from the junction, where a hideously steep trail (D2)—about as steep as the Huntington Ravine Trail—drops down to NH 26, coming out just east of the resort entrance.

1-1½ hours, 1-1.5 miles, total climb: 760'

Approach: *Park at the trailhead on NH 26, 0.4 miles west of the Balsams Resort entrance in Dixville Notch. See the Balsams Resort's Map & Guide.*

New England's Forests

A hundred years ago the forests of New Hampshire—most of New England, for that matter—were far less extensive than they are today. In 1860 New Hampshire was about 30% forest; today the figure is over 80%. The return of the forests has brought the return of many wild animals. For example, deer, bear, moose, coyotes and wild turkey, which we tend to take for granted, had been eliminated in many areas. Wild turkeys were re-introduced in Massachusetts in the 1970s, in northern areas, the moose population is growing rapidly and, recently, there have been several confirmed sightings of mountain lions.

This amazing comeback is due mainly to a shift in farming, away from the Northeast to the Midwest, and to the decline of wood products relative to petroleum products, but conservation forces have also played a role. For example, public outcry following devastating logging practices in the Zealand area, eventually led to the creation of the U.S. Forest Service and subsequently the White Mountain National Forest.

Most would agree that this is a fortunate trend. The northeastern United States is held up as proof that a large, highly industrialized population—70 million people live in or within a day's drive of New England—is not completely incompatible with an ecosystem which seems to be strongly on the rebound. The recent natural history of New England, indeed the eastern U.S., certainly gives hope to the claim that developed and "natural" environments can exist in close proximity—in fact intertwined—with each other. But with most of the prime land under strong development pressure, and with Maine being logged very aggressively—at least half of the state is owned by logging companies—the continuation of this recovery is not a given. The Northern Forest Project is an effort dedicated to protecting watershed, recreation, and wildlife habitats over a 26,000,000 acre extent of forested land from the Adirondacks, across northern Vermont and New Hampshire, and including more than half of Maine.

Photo opposite: Bob Grant; photo above: U.S. Forest Service

Mount Prospect 2,077'

Mount Prospect is located in **Weeks State Park**, a few miles south of Lancaster on US 3. The two main hiking options here are the **Around the Mountain Trail**, which does not go to the summit, and the **Mount Prospect Auto Road**, which does. The 3-mile loop of the Around the Mountain Trail circumnavigates the mountain near its base and passes through a variety of terrain, offering occasional viewpoints. The trail begins at the Mt. Prospect Ski Area and is also popular in winter with cross county skiers.

The Auto Road is open in the summer and fall to cars (a fee is charged), but is open for hiking and skiing year round. The grade over its 1.6 mile length is generally moderate and their are several good viewpoints along the way. The stone tower on the summit provides quite a fine view: the Presidentials lie to the southeast with Percy Peaks and the North Country forest to the northeast.

2 hours, 3.2 miles, total climb: 650' (Auto Road)
Approach: Park at the park entrance; it is located on US 3, 2.5 miles south of the (south) junction of Rts. 2 and 3 in Lancaster.
Maps: Weeks State Park - Mt. Prospect (Wilderness Map Company)

Mount Magalloway 3,360'

In an area of lower forested summits, Mount Magalloway seems to provide the best mountain views. The trail follows the old service road over mostly easy grades to the top. Take the trail behind the warden's cabin to the summit ledges. By climbing up onto the abandoned fire tower you will get fine, expansive views of the northern forest and mountains: in clear weather Maine's Aziscohos Lake and Rump Mountain (3,654'; trailless, wooded summit) are clearly visible. In the future, the Cohos Trail may loop across the summit.

1½ hours, 1.5 miles, total climb: 1,060'
Approach: Drive north on US Route 3 through Pittsburg 4.7 miles north of the dam at First Connecticut Lake, and turn right on a gravel road. Bear left at 2.2 miles and again at 2.9 miles, then right at 5.3 miles and 6.3 miles. Park at the end of this road, at 8.4 miles.
Maps: Magalloway Mountain (USGS); Topaz: NH Outdoor Recreation Map

Mount Monadnock 3,140' (Vermont)

Vermont's Mount Monadnock, in the extreme northeastern corner of the state, is a local landmark, rising over 2,000' above the Connecticut River. Although it is a fine hike on a good trail, Monadnock is almost unknown to hikers outside the area. From the bridge walk south along the highway about 100 feet and turn right onto a private road. This soon turns into a trail, and after a steep climb, crosses a stream (at about 45 minutes), then continues to climb before slackening and reaching the summit after about two hours. The trail is viewless until the top. Climb the tower (needs repair) to get above the trees for spectacular views of the North Country, into Canada, and south to Mount Washington and the Presidentials.

3½ hours and 5 miles roundtrip. Elevation gain: 2,100'

Approach: *Cross into Vermont from Colebrook and park immediately south of the Route 26 bridge on VT 102.*

Mont Mégantic 1105 m (Québec)

A circular, compact mountain of volcanic origin, Mégantic (3,624') rises abruptly out of the Québec farming country. Recently designated as a Provincial Park, Parc du Mont-Mégantic continues to be developed as a hiking and cross country skiing center. Although both the main summit and the adjacent summit of Mont Saint Joseph have roads up them, there is good hiking on this interesting mountain, and plans are in place to tie it to the Appalachian Trail in Maine. With good visibility, the Presidentials can be clearly seen, far away to the south. A free map is available at the lodge. There are campsites and cabins at the base.

Approach: *From the border (US Rt. 3), proceed north on Route 257 for 9 miles (through Chartierville), then right on Route 212 for 9 miles to Notre-Dame-des-Bois. Continue north (left) 4 miles to Route du Parc which leads to the park information center at the base.*

The Cohos Trail

The Cohos (pronounced "coe-ahhs") Trail is an approximately 160-mile hiking route which, when completed, will run from Barlett (Route 302, Crawford Notch) north to the Canadian border. Using a combination of existing trails, logging roads, old railroad beds, snowmobile trails and newly cut paths—about 90 percent of the right of way already existed in one form or another—the Cohos Trail (CT) provides a challenging and varied hiking right of way across a variety of terrain. At times mountainous, at times along lakes, at times through remote sections of forest, the Cohos Trail is an interesting addition to the options available to hikers in New Hampshire. In particular, the northern section, from Stark (Route 110) onward, opens a relatively seldom-visited area to long-distance and day hikers alike.

The guide book, *The Cohos Trail*, (Nicolin Fields Publishing, 2000) breaks the trail down into six sections, described below. Our map on page 91 gives a general idea of the hiking route; at present no detailed map of the trail exists.

1 - From Rt. 302, west of Bartlett village, the Cohos Trail starts out on **Davis Path** to Mt. Isolation, before heading west to Mt. Eisenhower to descend **Edmands Path** to Bretton Woods. From here it continues on various roads/trails to Zealand's campground.

2 - From **Zealand**, a few miles west of Bretton Woods, the trail heads north over Cherry Mountain (Mt. Martha and Owl's Head)—the detour to Cherry Pond is worthwhile—to **Jefferson**.

3 - From the tiny village of Jefferson (on Route 2), ascend Mt. Starr King and Mt. Waumbek and continue on the **Kilkenny Ridge Trail** over Cabot to Unknown Pond and Roger's Ledge to South Pond and NH 110, near the hamlet of Stark.

4 - From NH 110, the Cohos Trail plunges into the **Nash Stream Forest**, climbing both Percy Peaks and Sugarloaf. Continuing north, it traverses Mt. Muise and passes through Gadwah Notch, crossing a number of high mountain meadows along the way.

5 - Making use of snowmobile trails, the Cohos climbs Dixville Peak before descending to Balsams Resort in **Dixville Notch** on NH Route 26. After crossing Sanquinary Mtn., the route leads through moose country past Nathan Pond to Little Diamond Pond in **Coleman State Park**, the current (spring 2002) end of the Cohos Trail.

6 - From Coleman State Park, the trail strikes out across the high country of Stewartstown and Clarksville to **Pittsburg** and the **Connecticut Lakes**. From here northward the trail weaves along the shores of the several lakes and ends at the Canadian border.

Day Hikes along the Cohos Trail

The hikes described on the next few pages are offered as a way to introduce hikers to some of the terrain traversed by the Cohos Trail. The trips are presented from south to north.

Victor Head 2,265'

After crossing NH 110 near the hamlet of Stark, the Cohos Trail heads northwesterly, setting its sights on the Percy Peaks and Nash Stream Valley. Along the way it contours around the north side of Bald Mountain before eventually meeting the trail which comes up from Christine Lake. As a return option, consider following this trail (1.5 miles) down to **Christine Lake**—you can then walk back on the road to your starting point. Continuing, ascend past a huge glacial erractic to the short spur trail (right) which leads to the cliffs and great views on Victor Head. Return by the same route or via Christine Lake.

4 hours and 7 miles roundtrip. Elevation gain: 1,400'
Approach: Drive 9 miles east from Groveton on NH 110—or 15 miles west from Berlin—to Bell Hill Road. Take this to Percy Rd.; here bear left and continue a short distance to an orange gate.

Nash Bog

Nash Bog is the 200-acre lakebed—now a wetland—of the no longer existing Nash Bog Pond. In the summer of 1969, during a torrential rain storm, the dam burst, causing devastating flooding in Nash Stream Valley. This walk takes you upstream past boulders and flood rubble to today's peaceful Nash Bog, home to many species of birds and amphibious life forms. From the Sugarloaf Mtn. trailhead, walk down to the large bridge across Nash Stream, and then head upstream, keeping on the east side of the river. Let the Cohos Trail's yellow blazes guide you north for a little over a mile through a meadow, past a natural jacuzzi carved out of the streambed to the open spaces of Nash Bog. Here you can enjoy the view of the surrounding mountains, explore the bog, or just relax.

About 2 hours and 3 miles roundtrip.

Approach: Drive up Nash Stream Road 8.2 miles to the Sugarloaf Trailhead (see page 79) and park.

Fourth Connecticut Lake

Fourth Connecticut Lake—the smallest and northernmost in the series of Connecticut Lakes—is the source of the Connecticut River. From the border checkpoint, walk north along the road to pick up the boundary markers. Here head left (west), following the procession of markers in the actual border zone, a wide corridor cut in the forest. At 0.6 miles (10-15 minutes) turn left (south) on a signed path, and very soon you will come out of the woods at the Fourth Lake.

1 hours and 1.4 miles roundtrip. Elevation gain: 300'

Approach: Drive north from Pittsburg to the border crossing. Check in with at the border patrol and secure permission to park.

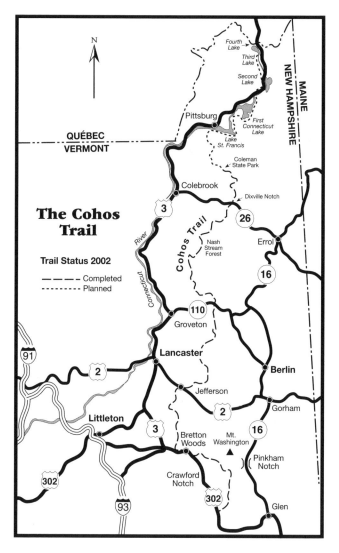

The Cohos Trail

Trail Status 2002

— — — Completed

········· Planned

N

QUÉBEC
VERMONT

Fourth Lake
Third Lake
Second Lake

MAINE
NEW HAMPSHIRE

Pittsburg

First Connecticut Lake

Lake St. Francis

Coleman State Park

Colebrook

Dixville Notch

26

Errol

Cohos Trail

Nash Stream Forest

16

Connecticut River

91

110

Groveton

2

Lancaster

Berlin

Jefferson

2

Gorham

Littleton

3

Bretton Woods

Mt. Washington

16

Pinkham Notch

302

Crawford Notch

302

93

Glen

7 Evans Notch

The Evans Notch area, often overlooked for the more popular Mount Washington Valley, deserves more consideration from serious hikers. Beautiful birch and pine stands, dramatic rock slabs and cliffs, and excellent campgrounds make this area a worthwhile destination. The Baldface Range runs along the Maine-New Hampshire border; it is the range to the east of the Carter Range. Although the summits are below the treeline, many of them are open, with views of mountains and lakes. In particular, the exciting circuit over North and South Baldface is outstanding. The loop hikes on Caribou and Speckled Mountains are also excellent. Evans Notch is accessed by NH–ME 113, which links US 2 (east of Gorham) to US 302, in Fryeburg, Maine.

Traverse of the Baldfaces

Similar to the much better known Franconia Ridge traverse, this is one of New England's finer mountain hikes, crossing the two highest mountains in the Baldface Range. A severe fire in 1903 opened up the view. Although the ridge is not as alpine in character as Franconia, the climb of South Baldface makes this a decidedly more difficult hike. The **Baldface Circle Trail** starts about 200' north of the parking area, and is easy going into **Circle Junction** at 0.7 mile. Head left, soon passing Slippery Brook Trail on the left, and begin the easy to moderate climb to **Baldface Shelter** (at 2.7 miles). The next section ascends steep granite slabs, with cracks in the smooth rock, detached blocks, and the occasional bush providing handholds. The grade eases, the views open up and, after crossing a minor summit, the top of **South Baldface** (3,569') is reached, 1.2 miles beyond the shelter. Superb views reward you from all directions, although nearby Carter Range blocks the Northern Presidentials. The mile-long traverse to **North Baldface** (3,591') is out in the open, with little protection from the elements. After North Baldface, more open walking leads past the Bicknell Ridge Trail to Eagle Link, where Baldface Circle Trail descends right, returning to Circle Junction and the road.

Hikers on South Baldface

Josh Stephen

Totals: 7 hours, 9.8 miles, climb: 3,540'
Approach: From Fryeburg, drive north 17.5 miles on Rt. 113 to the trail-head parking area (on the right), just beyond the AMC's Cold River Camp.

Basin Rim Outlook

Large fields border **Basin Pond**, providing an expansive, open feeling and a good view of the mountain wall that forms the rim. The **Basin Trail** begins at the parking area and runs along the south shore. After passing the end of the lake, the trail begins climbing, passes a loop side trail to **Hermit Falls**, and reaches the ridge and Rim Junction at 2.3 miles after a very steep finale. From here, it is possible to walk north or south along the rim edge on the **Basin Rim Trail**. To reach the outlook, take the Basin Rim Trail north (right) for about 0.1 mile to a spur trail (right) for a dramatic view of Basin Pond, 1,000 feet below. Return by the same route.

3 hours, 4.8 miles, total climb: 1,350'
Approach: The road into Basin Pond is on the west side of ME/NH 113, 19.5 miles north of Fryeburg.

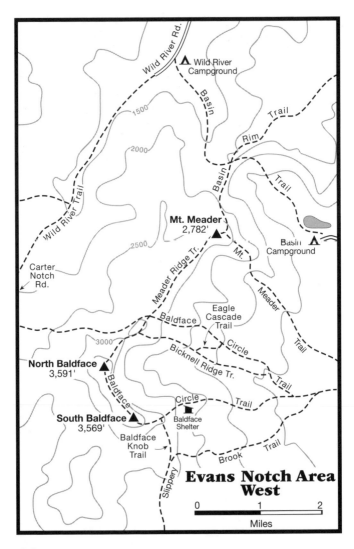

Wild River Rd.

△ Wild River
Campground

Basin

Trail

1500

Rim

2000

Basin

Trail

Wild River Trail

Mt. Meader
2,782' ▲

Basin
Campground △

Carter
Notch
Rd.

2500

Meader Ridge Tr.

Mt.

Meader

Baldface

Eagle
Cascade
Trail

Circle

3000

Bicknell Ridge Tr.

Trail

North Baldface ▲
3,591'

Baldface

Trail

Circle

South Baldface ▲
3,569'

Circle

Baldface
Shelter

Trail

Baldface
Knob
Trail

Brook

Trail

Slippery

**Evans Notch Area
West**

0   1   2

Miles

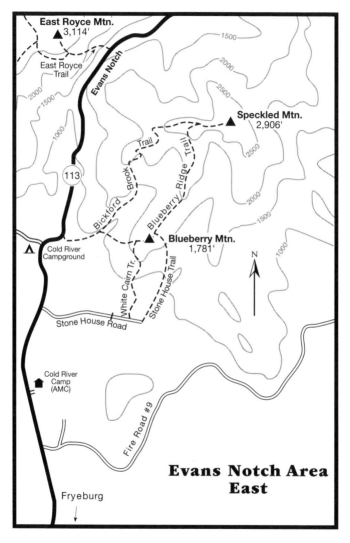

East Royce Mtn.
▲ 3,114'

East Royce
Trail

Evans Notch

1500

2000

2500

Speckled Mtn.
▲ 2,906'

2500

Trail

113

Bickford Brook

Blueberry Ridge Trail

2000

1500

1000

Blueberry Mtn.
▲ 1,781'

N

⛺ Cold River
Campground

White Cairn Tr.

Stone House Trail

Stone House Road

Cold River
Camp
(AMC)

Fire Road #9

**Evans Notch Area
East**

Fryeburg

East Royce Mountain 3,114'

The summit has an outlook with good views to the north and west. From Evans Notch, follow the **East Royce Trail** in a westerly direction as it climbs steeply, passing the Royce Connector Trail on the left after about a mile. Soon after, the trail runs across open ledges and at 1.4 miles reaches the south summit. The true summit is a short distance beyond. Continue on the short spur trail for good views to the west and north. Descend by the same route. Slightly higher **West Royce Mtn.** (3,116'), via the Connector and the Royce Trail, is 1.6 miles farther. Take the Royce Connector (0.2 mile) to the Royce Trail, which climbs the remaining 1.4 miles to its wooded summit.

2¾ hours, 3 miles, total climb: 1,700'

Approach: The trailhead for East Royce is in Evans Notch (ME 113), just north of the height of land.

The Roost 1,374'

This half-mile climb ascends steep and moderate grades to an overlook with granite slabs surrounded by blueberry bushes. You might see a bear when the berries are ripe. Look closely for the trailhead; it is literally just over the bridge, the sign nearly hidden in the trees. From the north trailhead, go up the wooden stairs and climb the narrow path to the top. Take the spur trail down a short way to the overlook where there are good views of the Wild River Valley, Evans Notch, the Carter Range, and more distant Mount Washington. The river below is a ribbon of salmon color. Return either by the same route or descend to the road on the south trail, which comes out just south of the Hastings Campground. It is then about 0.6 mile back to your starting point at the north trailhead.

1¼ hours, 1.8 miles (loop), total climb: 540'

Approach: The north trailhead is on Route 113, just north of Hastings Campground. Park just before the bridge, walk over it, and look on the right for the sign and trail.

Wilderness Areas

Five regions within the White Mountain National Forest, totaling about 115,000 acres, have been designated by Congress as wilderness areas. These areas have trails and are open to the public—the Pemigewasset Wilderness, for example receives heavy use—but they are regulated to preserve their primitive, natural state. No vehicles are allowed, including bicycles. Logging is not permitted but is in the rest of the National Forest. Pre-existing shelters are either removed or simply allowed to decay. Camping is permitted, but must conform to special rules in order to minimize impact. See the box on low impact hiking, page 99.

The Forest Service does provide trail signs in wilderness areas, but in a minimal fashion. For example, mileages are not generally given. Trails are maintained, but not usually to the standard elsewhere on the forest.

Unlike wilderness areas in the western U.S. where primitive land is selected for preservation, our wild areas are wild by decree—the land may have been heavily logged in the past. The intent is to encourage and allow the land over time to return to a natural, more "original" state.

Caribou Mountain 2,850'

Caribou is an attractive mountain with a rocky, barren summit. Perhaps the most interesting way to climb it is as a loop hike. Ascend the **Caribou Trail**, passing **Kees Falls** at about 2 miles, and reaching the col between Gammon Mtn. and Caribou Mountain at about 3 miles. Here, turn right on the **Mud Brook Trail**, following it to the broad, open summit with its superb views. From the top it is 3 miles back to your starting point via Mud Brook Trail. Most of the route lies in the **Caribou-Speckled Mountain Wilderness**.

4¼ hours, 6.7 miles (loop), total climb: 1,920'
Approach: The trailhead is on Route 113, 6 miles north of the AMC's Cold River Camp, on the right.

Speckled Mountain   2,906'

Speckled Mountain, the highest mountain on the east side of the Evans Notch highway, offers magnificent views from open ledges. From the top there is an unobstructed panorama of the Maine and New Hampshire landscape. From **Brickett Place** (a well-preserved brick dwelling from the 1800s), follow the **Bickford Brook Trail** (via Ames Mtn.) for 4.3 miles to the summit of Speckled Mountain, passing some interesting water slides and rocks part way up. To return via the **Blueberry Ridge Trail**, leave Bickford Brook Trail (left) 0.5 mile below the summit, passing the Stone House and White Cairn Trails about 2.7 and 2.9 miles from the top, respectively. The open, ledgy summit of Blueberry Mountain has good views and is a worthwhile hiking destination in its own right (see below). Continue the descent, rejoining the Bickford Brook Trail 0.6 mile above Brickett Place.

   5½ hours, 8.6 miles (loop), total climb: 2,500'
   Approach: *About 2.6 miles north of Cold River Campground turn right off NH-ME 113 and park at the Brickett Place.*

Blueberry Mountain   1,781'

This is an interesting, not overly demanding hike to the open areas on Blueberry Mountain's summit. From the gate on Stone House Road, continue on the road for about 0.3 mile to the **White Cairn Trail** on the left. Take this and after about an hour of climbing, reach the **Blueberry Ridge Trail**. Soon after, pick up the 0.5-mile overlook loop for great views. This comes out near the **Stone House Trail**, which is just below the summit of Blueberry Mountain. Amble around on the summit, a large, open, ledgy area. The Stone House Trail descends over some steep sections to the road (1.5 miles from summit to road). Turn right and walk for about a half mile to reach the gate you started from.

   2½ hours, 3.8 miles (loop), total climb: 1,200'
   Approach: *A little over a mile north of AMC's Cold River Camp, turn right on Stone House Road, and follow it to the gate, about a mile farther on.*

Low Impact Hiking

In most areas of our lives, we want to make an impact. Not when camping or hiking! The backcountry is easily damaged. Otherwise well-meaning hikers walk or camp on arctic vegetation, unknowingly pollute drinking water, or destroy small trees for campfires or to clear a tentsite.

Low impact means just what it says: disturbing as little as possible the natural areas we hike in and enjoy. Here are some tips:

Take only pictures, leave only footprints; carry out all that you bring in; if you see trash, cart it out; never make camp above treeline or camp, bathe, wash dishes, or deposit human waste within 200 feet of a stream, pond, or trail; use a campstove instead of fires; don't reuse campsites, except in designated areas; use outhouses if available; if not, bury human and pet waste in a hole at least five inches deep, with a minimal amount of toilet paper; and try to hike without leaving any trace of your visit. Try to hike with the goal of leaving an area in better shape than you found it. And be especially cautious above treeline; one step of a hiker's boot can kill fragile arctic plants. Some arctic flowers take many years to bloom. Keep on the trail or step only on rocks.

Maps: AMC: #5 *Carter Range-Evans Notch*; DeLorme; Map Adventures; USGS: *Chatham, Speckled Mtn., Wild River.*

Campgrounds: *The Forest Service maintains four campgrounds in the Evans Notch area: Hastings, Wild River, Basin Pond, and Cold River. Contact the Evans Notch District Office in Bethel, Maine for information.*

8 | Jackson and North Conway

Although most of the hiking activity is on nearby Mount Washington and the Presidential Range, the immediate Jackson–North Conway area has plenty to recommend it. In particular, the Moats and a well-known landmark, Kearsarge North, offer excellent trips with spectacular views. Jackson's distinctive pair of summits, North and South Doublehead, are favorite hiking and skiing destinations. And for climbers the steep granite of Whitehorse and Cathedral Ledges provides some of the best climbing in the eastern United States.

North Moat (3,201') and Red Ridge

North Moat is one of the lower summits described in our guide, but about one third of this 10-mile hike is across open ledges, and the views are superb! From the parking area, take the **Moat Mountain Trail** past the interesting pools and granite boulders of **Diana's Baths** (at 0.5 mile) and continue for 1.1 miles before turning left onto **Red Ridge Trail**. Note that Diana's Baths is a very popular hike and has recently been made wheelchair accessible. After another mile, cross a road and bear right along Moat Brook before ascending the wide, low-angle ledges of Red Ridge, meeting the Moat Mountain Trail again at 4.7 miles. Now head north (right) over terrain that alternates between ledge and forest to the top of North Moat at 5.9 miles. From here on a clear day, it is possible to see the ocean, about 50 miles distant. From the summit, continue north, descending (at times steeply) numerous open or semi-open ledges and slabs to Lucy Brook, where the Attitash Trail comes in from the left. Continue (right) on Moat Mountain Trail over easy terrain back past Diana's Baths to your starting point. The route is equally fine when done in the opposite direction: Some may prefer tackling North Moat first, as it is steeper than Red Ridge.

7 hours, 10.2 miles, total climb: 2,900'
Approach: From the traffic light at the north end of North Conway, drive west on River Road, then bear right on West Side Road for about 2 miles to the trailhead on the left.

Whitehorse Ledge and North Moat Mountain   Ned Therrien

Whitehorse Ledge

The steep slabs of Whitehorse Ledge and adjacent Cathedral Ledge offer the rock climber hundreds of routes with all levels of difficulty. A variety of trails makes it quite easy for non-climbers to observe the scene. There is even a road to the top of Cathedral Ledge. From the trailhead at **Echo Lake State Park**, start on the lake circuit trail, branching left after about 0.4 mile. After crossing two minor trails, bear left at the trail junction at 0.7 mile. At the next junction, 0.3 mile farther on, head left to climb Whitehorse; the trail to **Cathedral Ledge** is straight ahead. Continue, ascending steeply, reaching a good viewpoint of the climbing area after another half mile. The top, with a view of Moat Mountain, is 0.1 mile farther on. Return by the same route or complete the circuit of Whitehorse. Have a look at the map sign in the parking lot.

2 hours, 3.2 miles, total climb: 1,000'

Approach: At the north end of North Conway (at the traffic light), drive west on River Road, following signs to Echo Lake State Park.

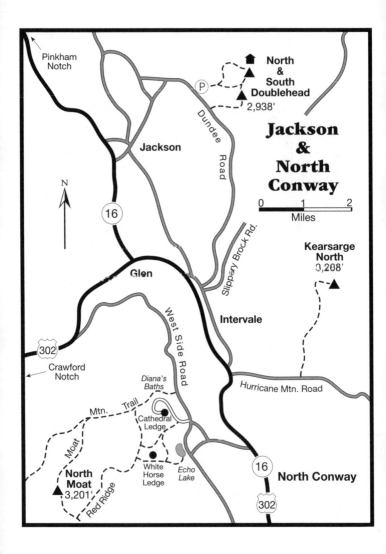

Pinkham
Notch

North
&
South
Doublehead
2,938'

P

Dundee Road

Jackson

**Jackson
&
North
Conway**

N

16

0   1   2
Miles

Kearsarge
North
3,268'

Glen

Slippery Brock Rd.

Intervale

302

Crawford
Notch

West Side Road

Hurricane Mtn. Road

Diana's
Baths

Mtn.   Trail

Moat

Cathedral
Ledge

Echo
Lake

16

North Conway

North
Moat
3,201'

White
Horse
Ledge

Red Ridge

302

Kearsarge North 3,268'

This popular, solid hike takes you to an open summit only 15 air miles from Mount Washington. As you reach the top, dramatic views of Tuckerman Ravine and the lakes of western Maine greet you. Clamber up the old firetower for the full view. Starting out as an old road, the **Kearsarge North** trail gets rockier and steeper after about a half mile. As it climbs through woods and across intermittent ledges it provides good views of the Saco Valley. After gaining the main ridge the trail swings to the east, making the final push to the top from the north. Descend by the same route.

4½ hours, 6.2 miles, total climb: 2,600'

Approach: *From Intervale, north of North Conway, drive 1.5 miles east on Hurricane Mountain Road to the trailhead on the left.*

Nearby **Black Cap Mountain** (2,370') has an excellent view from its bare summit. Popular with kids, the 1.1-mile trail (700'-climb) starts on Hurricane Mtn. Rd., 3.7 miles from NH 16 in Intervale.

North and South Doublehead

This route first ascends South Doublehead (2,938'), with views of the North Conway area, before continuing to the stylish log cabin on top of North Doublehead (3,053'). The cabin can be rented; contact the Saco Ranger Station in Conway. From Dundee Rd., follow **New Path**, first across easy terrain, then up very steeply, reaching the top of South Doublehead at 1.4 miles. Now drop into the col—**Old Path** appears from the left—and continue to North Doublehead, at 1.8 miles. There are views of Mt. Washington's ravines and an unusual view of deep Carter Notch. From the top, stroll down the wide and pleasantly graded **Doublehead Ski Trail**. Complete the loop by heading left up the road.

2½ hours, 4 miles, total climb: 1,750'

Approach: *From the covered bridge in Jackson, drive up Route 16B to Dundee Rd., bear right, and continue to the height of land, 3.4 miles total. Doublehead Ski Trail and Old Path start 0.5 mile below New Path.*

Campgrounds: *Private campgrounds in North Conway, Glen, and Bartlett.*

9 Crawford Notch and Zealand

One of New Hampshire's most impressive physical features, Crawford Notch is approached from the west across a mountain-ringed basin. Upon reaching the notch, the highway squeezes through a narrow rock portal, suddenly revealing a huge glacial valley below. The road drops steeply, passing several cascades, and mountainsides two and three thousand feet high form the valley walls. Closely linked to Crawford is the Zealand area, with Zealand Falls Hut and access to classic routes like the traverse of the Bonds and the demanding Twinway trail over South Twin to Galehead Hut. About a dozen 4,000'-ers are in the area. In winter there is plenty of snowshoeing, ice climbing, and nordic skiing. The AMC Hiker Shuttle connects the Crawford-Zealand area with Pinkham and Franconia Notch during the summer and fall months. When approaching from the south, exit I-93 at Franconia Notch and proceed north on US 3 to Twin Mountain. Crawford Notch is then nine miles east on US 302.

Crawford Path to Mizpah Spring Hut

This moderate hike to AMC's Mizpah Spring Hut can easily be extended to include **Mount Clinton** (4,310'). From the trailhead on Mt. Clinton Road, climb moderately on Crawford Path to **Mizpah Cut-off** (1.7 miles). Head right on it for 0.7 mile to **Webster Cliff Trail**. Then bear left, reaching the hut in a few minutes. Total distance from the car: 2.5 miles. Either return the same way or via Mt. Clinton (also called Mt. Pierce). To do the latter, continue north on Webster Cliff Trail, reaching the open summit of Clinton after about 0.8 mile. And to continue on the loop, head north for about 5 minutes to reach Crawford Path. Here turn left and stay on Crawford Path back to the highway, a distance of 2.9 miles. Crawford Path was the first trail to the top of Mt. Washington—it is one of the oldest hiking trails in the United States.

4–5 hours, 6.2 miles, total climb: 2,400' (Mt. Clinton loop)
Approach: Crawford Path begins on US 302, but the nearby hiker parking area on Mt. Clinton Road is the best place to start.

Mt. Webster and Crawford Notch from Mt. Willard   Robert Kozlow

Mount Jackson 4,052'

The top of Mount Jackson is rocky and open, with good views in all directions, especially south toward Mount Field and the Zealand area. From the highway, follow the **Webster-Jackson Trail** as it climbs steeply (but with occasional short dips) past Elephant Head and Bugle Cliff (There are good views from these cliffs.), reaching a trail junction at 1.4 miles. Take the Jackson branch left and climb steadily to the summit, finishing on some steep ledges. Return by the same route, or by the variation described below.

> *4 hours, 5.2 miles, total climb: 2,200'*
>
> ***Approach:*** *The Webster-Jackson Trail begins at the east end of Saco Lake in Crawford Notch.*

Variation: For a loop including both **Webster** and **Jackson**, ascend Jackson, then head south on **Webster Cliff Trail**, reaching the summit of Mount Webster (3,910') after 1.4 miles, where there are views into **Crawford Notch**. Then retrace your steps to the Webster Branch of the Jackson-Webster Trail and descend (left) to Crawford Notch. Total distance for this loop is 6.4 miles.

Mount Webster (3,910') via Webster Cliff

From the highway the **Webster Cliff Trail** climbs up the steep southern side of Mount Webster, reaching the first good viewpoint at 1.8 miles. The trail then works its way up and along the top of Webster Cliff with a number of clifftop views down into Crawford Notch and across to Mount Willey. You reach the rocky summit of Webster at 3.3 miles. From here the open summit of Mount Jackson is an easy 1.4 miles farther on. Beyond Mount Jackson the Webster Cliff Trail continues to Mizpah Spring Hut (5.7 miles from the highway) and ends at **Crawford Path** after 6.7 miles. For the hike described here, descend steeply from Jackson's summit on the **Webster–Jackson Trail**, reaching Crawford Notch after 2.6 miles. Arrange a car for the four-mile road section back to your starting point at the Webster Cliff trailhead on US 302.

6 hours, 7.3 miles, total climb: 3,100'

Approach: Webster Cliff Trail starts on the east side of US 302, four miles south of Crawford Notch

It is also possible to descend directly to Crawford Notch from Mt. Webster by taking the Webster Branch of the Webster-Jackson Trail, shortening the above trip by 1.4 miles and about one hour.

Traverse of the Southern Presidentials

The long southern ridge of Mount Washington, which includes the summits of Monroe, Franklin, Eisenhower, Clinton, and Jackson, ends at Crawford Notch and forms good material for a two-day hike. For example, from Crawford Notch via Crawford Path it is a moderate day (5–6 hours walking, 6.8 miles) in high alpine terrain to the Lakes of the Clouds Hut. One can then climb Mount Washington the following day, return to the hut, and descend the Ammonoosuc Ravine Trail. Time and distance from Crawford Notch to the base of Ammonoosuc Ravine: 2 days, 13 miles, including the climb of Mount Washington.

Hiker Facilities at Crawford Notch

Reminders of bygone days, the picturesque old train depot, known as **Crawford's**, and another historic structure, now known as the **Crawford Notch Hostel**, serve hikers and other visitors to the area. The buildings are located 4 miles east of Bretton Woods on US 302 at the height of land in Crawford Notch. The Depot is a staffed information center; it sells maps, books, and snacks. The hostel, which is open year round, provides rustic accommodations for 24, with two rooms of bunks. Guests bring their own food and sleeping bags. A complete kitchen with stove and refrigerator is available. The hostel has toilets and showers. The AMC hiker shuttle services the trailheads in the area. For more information, contact the Appalachian Mountain Club. By spring 2003, the AMC plans to have a new educational facility completed: The Highland Center at Crawford Notch will be able to accommodate 120 guests.

Mount Willey 4,285'

Unless perhaps you've just returned from the Rockies, the sweeping 3,000'-high east flank of Mount Willey, as seen from the top of Crawford Notch, will impress you. No lowly eastern hill, this. Unfortunately, no trail directly ascends this magnificent slope. Our route climbs the southeast ridge. From **Willey House Site**, follow **Kedron Flume Trail** to **Ethan Pond Trail** at 1.3 miles and bear right to reach the **Willey Range Trail** at 1.6 miles, and Mount Willey's summit after another 1.1 miles. The upper portion of Kedron Flume Trail is quite steep, as is much of the Willey Range Trail, which resorts to ladder-steps about half-way up. The best viewpoint is just below the summit, with good views to the east and north. Return by the same route or by the variation described below. The map in Chapter 10 shows this hike.

5 hours, 5.4 miles, total climb: 2,900'
Approach: *Willey House Site is 2.5 miles south of Crawford Notch.*

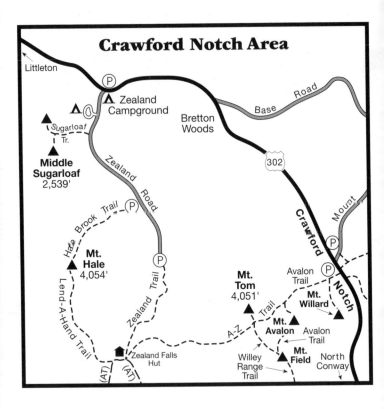

Crawford Notch Area

Littleton

Zealand Campground

Bretton Woods

Base Road

302

Crawford Notch

Mount

Sugarloaf Tr.

Middle Sugarloaf 2,539'

Zealand Road

Hale Brook Trail

Mt. Hale 4,054'

Lend-A-Hand Trail

Zealand Trail

Zealand Falls Hut

(AT)   (AT)

Mt. Tom 4,051'

A-Z Trail

Avalon Trail

Mt. Willard

Mt. Avalon

Avalon Trail

Willey Range Trail

Mt. Field

North Conway

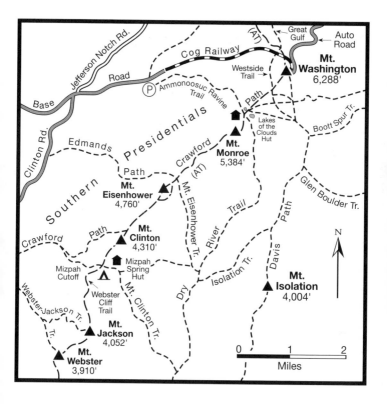

Great Gulf

Auto Road

Jefferson Notch Rd.

Cog Railway (AT)

Base Road

(P) Ammonoosuc Ravine Trail

Westside Trail

Mt. Washington 6,288'

Clinton Rd.

Edmands

Presidentials

Path

Crawford (AT)

Lakes of the Clouds Hut

Mt. Monroe 5,384'

Boott Spur Tr.

Southern

Mt. Eisenhower 4,760'

Mt. Eisenhower Tr.

River Trail

Glen Boulder Tr.

Crawford Path

Mt. Clinton 4,310'

Mizpah Cutoff

Mizpah Spring Hut

Webster Cliff Trail

Dry

Isolation Tr.

Davis Path

Mt. Isolation 4,004'

N

Webster-Jackson Tr.

Mt. Clinton Tr.

Mt. Jackson 4,052'

Mt. Webster 3,910'

0   1   2
Miles

Variation on Mount Willey hike: From the top of Willey, continue 1.4 miles on **Willey Range Trail** to **Mt. Field**, at 4,326' the highest point of the ridge. The views are restricted. About 100 yards north, head right on the **Avalon Trail** and descend quite directly passing the **A–Z Trail** junction (left), and continuing to Crawford Notch and the train depot. The short side trip (right) to **Mt. Avalon's** spectacular outlook is well worth the effort. Coordinate your transportation from Crawford Notch back to Willey House Site.

6 hours, 8.6 miles, elevation gain: 3,220'

Ripley Falls

This short, popular hike leads to a 100' waterfall. Take the **Ethan Pond Trail** from the parking area, and branch left onto **Arethusa-Ripley Falls Trail** after 0.2 mile. You reach the base of Ripley Falls after another 0.3 mile. The Arethusa-Ripley Falls Trail continues to **Arethusa Falls**, the more impressive of the two falls. See Chapter 10 for the hike description for Arethusa Falls and Frankenstein Cliff. Try to visit these falls in the spring or after a good rain when the streams have a good volume of water.

1 hour, 1 mile, elevation gain: 300'

Approach: Park on the short side road off US 302, about a mile south of Willey House Site.

Mount Willard   2,850'

For a short hike on easy terrain that leads to a dramatic view, Willard is hard to beat (see photo). Part of the trail coincides with an old carriage road, making for excellent walking. From Crawford's, start on **Avalon Trail**, but branch left after only 0.1 mile on **Mount Willard Trail**, which leads to clifftop ledges high above the U-shaped glacial valley that forms Crawford Notch. You are safe enough if you stay well away from the edge, but as there is no protection from the dropoff, be careful here with children or if conditions are wet or icy. Return by the same route.

1¾ hours, 2.8 miles, total climb: 925'

Approach: Park at Crawford's (the old train depot) in Crawford Notch, cross the tracks, and pick up the Avalon Trail.

Mount Field (4,326') and Mount Avalon

Cross the tracks behind Crawford Depot and take the **Avalon Trail**. After 1.3 miles of moderate climbing, Avalon Trail turns sharply left (the A-Z Trail continues straight) and climbs, at times extremely steeply, to a saddle just below Mount Avalon (3,442'). Take the short spur trail (left) to the top for really fine views of the Crawford Notch area (best views on this hike). Return to the main trail, which after an easy section, climbs steadily to meet the **Willey Range Trail** just north of the summit of Mount Field (limited views). To continue with the loop, descend the Willey Range Trail to the Tom-Field saddle and head right on the **A-Z Trail**, and then the Avalon Trail, to return to Crawford Depot.

4½ hours, 5 miles, total climb: 2,500'
Approach: From Crawford Depot in Crawford Notch.

Mount Tom (4,051') is easily climbed from the Tom–Field saddle as a variation on the above route (adds 45 minutes. and 1.2 miles). Starting from Crawford Depot, take the Avalon and A–Z Trails to the saddle, and then **Mount Tom Spur** (right) to the top (views).

4 hours, 5.8 miles, total climb: 2,150' (Mt. Tom only)
Approach: From Crawford Depot in Crawford Notch.

Mount Hale   4,054'

A beautiful, partly open summit and visit to Zealand Falls Hut are the attractions of this loop trip. From the trailhead indicated below, climb Mount Hale on the pleasant and wooded **Hale Brook Trail**, reaching the top after 2.4 miles. The partial view south across nearby Zealand Notch to Mount Carrigain and Carrigain Notch is impressive. Hopefully the atmosphere will cooperate, allowing you to take in the entire sweep of mountains from Washington to Carrigain. To the west you look up at nearby North and South Twin. Descend 2.5-mile **Lend-a-Hand Trail** through interesting and varied forest, heading left on Twinway the last few feet to Zealand Falls Hut. From the hut, take Twinway and **Zealand Trail** back to Zealand Road, and walk the mile down the road.

6 hours, 8.5 miles, elevation gain: 2,350'
Approach: The trailhead is on Zealand Road, 2.5 miles from Route 302.

Mount Carrigain from Zeacliff   Ed Rolfe

North and Middle Sugarloaf (2,539')

Thanks to a forest fire many years ago, Middle Sugarloaf and North Sugarloaf are bare summits and offer great views. Starting out quite gently, the **Sugarloaf Trail** soon steepens before attaining the col between North and Middle Sugarloaf. Since the view is better from Middle, we head left, making the final push to the top for a total climb of about 900'. You can see most of the Presidential Range from here, even Mount Adams, far to the north. Somewhat lower North Sugarloaf (2,310') gives a slightly different perspective and adds about 0.5 mile to the trip. The trail to North Sugarloaf crosses a pegmatite dike where quartz and mica crystals can be collected. Both North and Middle Sugarloaf are quite prominent from US 302.

2 hours, 2.8 miles, elevation gain: 900'

Approach: The trailhead is on Zealand Road, one mile from Route 302 and just past the Forest Service's Sugarloaf Campgrounds.

Zealand Falls Hut

The front porch vista of the cliffs above Zealand Notch and of more distant Carrigain Notch is considered by some to be the best view from any of the AMC huts. Water cascades over pale granite slabs just outside the door of this gem, ably run by AMC staff. The hut is 2.7 miles from **Zealand Road** (south off US 302, 2.3 miles east of Twin Mountain). Park at the end of the 3.7-mile road, and take **Zealand Trail** over gently ascending terrain. Head right on **Twinway** for the last 0.2 mile. Zealand Hut is open (caretaker basis) during the winter, and is very popular with skiers and snowshoers—weekends are heavily booked. Zealand Rd. is not plowed.

Zealand Falls Hut to Galehead Hut

Overnighting at Zealand and Galehead Huts gives a fine introduction to "hut-to-hut" hiking. The 7-mile **Twinway** links Zealand Falls Hut with Galehead Hut, but only after a traverse of both **Zealand Mountain** (4,260') and **South Twin** (4,902'). From the hut, ascend steadily through a birch forest, coming out into the open at 1.2 miles. Here, take the short side trail left to incomparable **Zeacliff**: The mountainside falls away precipitously at your feet, and out of the void rises the wild, yet graceful ridgeline of Mount Carrigain. In June, magenta rhododendron blossoms complete the magic of this spot. At 3 miles, a 0.1-mile spur trail (right) leads to the viewless top of Zealand Mtn. At 4 miles break into the high, open terrain on Mount Guyot (4,580') and pass **Bondcliff Trail** on the left. (Chapter 12 describes the traverse of the Bonds.) Finally, at 6.2 miles, the summit of South Twin is yours. Great panoramic views! From here the trail plunges downward to Galehead Hut.

5 hours, 7 miles, elevation gain: 2,300'
Approach: *Trailhead parking for Zealand Falls Hut is at the end of Zealand Road, 3.7 miles from US 302. See Zealand Falls Hut, above.*

Galehead Hut and South Twin (4,902')

Although this is a somewhat long and arduous excursion, energetic peakbaggers may want to add **Galehead Mtn.** (4,024') and possibly even **North Twin** (4,761') to their lists. Starting near the trailhead for Mount Garfield, the **Gale River Trail** first leads over easy ground, then steepens, climbing stone steps to reach the main ridge and **Garfield Ridge Trail** (AT). This is an excellent trail, and the hike to Galehead Hut (4.6 miles) is a popular and worthwhile destination in its own right. The route up South Twin (on **Twinway**) is steep and very direct, reaching the spectacular, open summit 0.8 mile from Galehead Hut. The view to the north is limited by North Twin, but the views along Garfield Ridge to Franconia Ridge, into the Pemigewasset Basin, along the ridgeback of the Bonds, and east to Mount Carrigain are unsurpassed.

8 hours, 11 miles, elevation gain: 3,330'

Approach: From I-93, drive 5.5 miles north on US 3 to Gale River Road, opposite Trudeau Rd. Turn right and continue 1.6 miles to parking.

Galehead Mountain (4,024') is a 20-minute walk on the **Frost Trail** from Galehead Hut. There are very limited views from the top.

North Twin   4,761'

The **North Twin Trail**, which starts on old railroad grades, ascends a pleasant wooded valley, crossing and recrossing Little River. (Crossing the stream will be difficult during heavy runoff.) At about the halfway point, the trail bears right and gets serious—there's still about 2,000' of climbing ahead. Just below the summit you are rewarded with a fine view of Mt. Washington. The actual summit of North Twin offers no views, but a short spur trail to the right opens things up with views toward Franconia Ridge, Mount Garfield and, far below, Galehead Hut. Return by the same route.

6–7 hours, 8.8 miles, elevation gain: 3,000'

Approach: Drive 8.5 miles north on US 3 from I-93. Turn right and proceed to the end of Haystack Road (2.5 miles).

Maps: Wilderness: *Crawford Notch;* Map Adventures; USGS: *Crawford Notch, So. Twin Mtn.;* AMC #2; Crawford Notch State Park map.

Camping: Forest Service: *Zealand Rd. and at Dry River (south of Crawford Notch). Private campgrounds in Twin Mountain and Bethlehem.*

10 Mount Carrigain and Dry River Region

The impressive, isolated peak of Mount Carrigain and 200-foot Arethusa Falls—New Hampshire's highest—are two of the attractions of this area. On both sides of Route 302 popular hikes lead to various summits and waterfalls. After dropping steeply out of Crawford Notch, Route 302 passes a number of important trailheads. Davis Path and the Dry River Trail lead north to Mount Washington as does Webster Cliff Trail which carries the AT on its northward journey. Mount Carrigain is easily recognized from most of the White Mountain summits, thus it is no surprise that most of the major summits are visible from Carrigain.

Mount Carrigain (4,680') via Signal Ridge

Hikers who make the relatively long trek up Mount Carrigain— and 14th highest in New Hampshire—will experience a distinct feeling of isolation. The observation deck gets you above the trees, and you can study the panoramic view to your heart's content. The long, forested approach is reminiscent of the Adirondacks. From the parking area, the **Signal Ridge Trail** starts along a rushing brook, meeting the **Carrigain Notch Trail** in a swampy area after 1.7 miles. Continue straight, staying on Signal Ridge Trail, and soon the climb up the ridge gets underway. This is a long climb, but there are good intermittent views, especially when the leaves are off the trees! At 4.5 miles you come onto the open ridge and can see the top, now only a half mile away. The final climb to the summit is in dense woods. Descend by the same route.

> *6½ hours, 10 miles, total climb: 3,250'*
> *Approach: From Bartlett, drive north 3.7 miles on US 302 to Sawyer River Road, then left for 2 miles to the trailhead.*

Carrigain Notch variation: From the summit, descend the **Desolation Trail** (precipitously steep, but with good footing) reaching **Carrigain Notch Trail** after 1.9 miles. Head right over very easy terrain, eventually passing through Carrigain Notch (there is not much in the way of a view) and returning to the Signal Ridge Trail after 7 miles' walking from the summit.

Total distance for this loop is about 13.5 miles.

Signal Ridge Trail on Mount Carrigain   Robert Kozlow

Mount Tremont 3,384'

Visitors to the upper slopes of Mount Tremont get a rare treat—a virgin stand of huge red spruce. And although the entire trail is in forest, the summit has great views of Washington, Chocorua, and Carrigain, including a wide view of the mountains to the south: Hancock, Tripyramid, Osceola, Tecumseh, and others. The **Mount Tremont Trail** starts out gently on a logging road, paralleling a brook. About halfway, the angle of the trail increases, and the upper section is quite steep. Descend by the same route.

5 hours, 5.6 miles, total climb: 2,500'

Approach: The trailhead is three miles west of Bartlett on US 302, on the left side of the road.

Arethusa Falls and Frankenstein Cliff

This loop hike takes you to the state's highest waterfall, 200' Arethusa Falls, and along the top of an 800' cliff. The well-marked trail ascends through beautiful white birches and across steep wooded slopes, leading you up Bemis Brook to the falls, about 1.5 miles and an hour in from the road. In the spring, or after a good rain, Arethusa is an impressive cascading waterfall. In leaner periods it's much less impressive. To do the loop hike climb (right) past the falls on the **Arethusa-Ripley Trail**. After a mile pick up **Frankenstein Cliff Trail** (Arethusa-Ripley Trail heads left to Ripley Falls) and soon you begin the traverse across the top of the cliff, passing various viewpoints before dropping very steeply into the valley. After walking under the steel arches of the RR bridge, bear right and return to the parking area.

4 hours, 4.3 miles, 1,500' of climbing

Approach: Park at the end of the short access road, on the west side of US 302, six miles south of Crawford Notch.

Nancy Pond

A 300'-high cascade and a secluded wilderness pond are the rewards of this hike. Yellow-blazed **Nancy Pond Trail** starts on gentle terrain, making several stream crossings. At 1.5 miles it crosses Nancy Brook; this can be difficult during heavy run-off. Continue climbing, and after negotiating some loose, gravelly sections of trail (old landslides), reach the base of **Nancy Cascades** at 2.4 miles. The cascade culminates with a waterfall into a beautiful, clear pool. From here the trail ascends steeply, giving more views of water and of mountains across the highway. The trail leads through a virgin spruce forest before skirting the north shore of **Nancy Pond**. If you continue past Nancy Pond for ¾ mile to the dam at the far end of Norcross Pond, you'll gain a fine view of Mount Bond. Return by the same trail.

5 hours, 7 miles, elevation gain: 2,200'

Approach: The trailhead is five miles west of Bartlett on US 302.

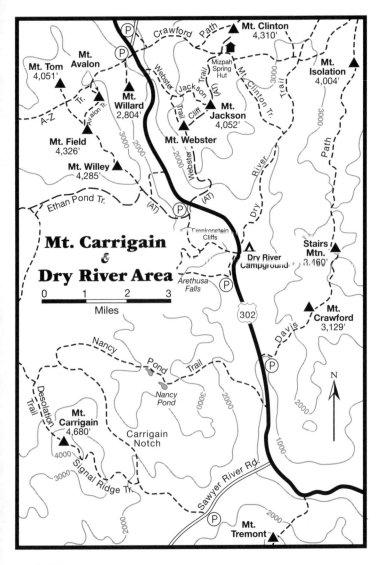

Mt. Carrigain
&
Dry River Area

0   1   2   3
Miles

Mt. Tom
4,051'

Mt. Avalon

A-Z Tr.

Avalon Tr.

Mt. Willard
2,804'

Crawford Path

Webster Trail

Jackson Trail (AT)

Mt. Clinton
4,310'

Mizpah
Spring Hut

Mt. Isolation
4,004'

Mt. Clinton Tr.

Mt. Jackson
4,052'

Cliff

Mt. Webster

Mt. Field
4,326'

Mt. Willey
4,285'

Webster

Ethan Pond Tr.

(AT)

(AT)

Dry River

Dry River Trail Path

Frankenstein Cliffs

Dry River Campground

Arethusa Falls

Stairs Mtn.
3,460'

302

Mt. Crawford
3,129'

Davis

Nancy Pond Trail

Pond

Nancy Pond

Mt. Carrigain
4,680'

Desolation Trail

Signal Ridge Tr.

Carrigain Notch

Sawyer River Rd.

N

Mt. Tremont

Dry River Trail

To the west of Davis Path is a route of almost equal length, the Dry River Trail. From its trailhead on Route 302, just north of the Forest Service's Dry River Campground, it passes through the forest of the Presidential-Dry River Wilderness, ultimately ascending the steep flank of Oakes Gulf to end at **Lakes of the Clouds Hut**, 9.6 miles from its starting point. At 3 miles, **Mount Clinton Trail** branches left to **Mizpah Spring Hut**. (on Crawford Path). A good excursion is to hike 5.4 miles up the trail to a side trail that drops down to the pool below Dry River Falls—this makes for good swimming spot on a hot day. The Dry River Trail also provides a route to Mount Isolation, either as an ascent or descent option.

Mount Crawford (3,129') via Davis Path

The lower summits traversed by Davis Path offer some of the finer views in the region. From the parking area, cross the Saco River on a suspension bridge and hike up an old bridle path, obtaining the ridge at 1.7 miles. At 2.2 miles, the spur trail (0.3 mile) to the summit of Mount Crawford branches left. The views from the rocky summit are excellent: Crawford Notch, the Dry River Valley, Mount Carrigain, and its neighbors. Return the same way.

4½ hours, 5 miles, total climb: 2,100'

Approach: Trailhead parking for Davis Path is on US 302, 6 miles from Bartlett, across from Notchland Inn.

Campgrounds: Forest Service: Dry River; Zealand and Sugarloaf. Private campgrounds along US 302 in Bartlett, Glen, Twin Mountain, and in Bethlehem. The AMC runs a hostel in Crawford Notch.

Maps: AMC #3: Crawford Notch-Sandwich Range; Map Adventures: White Mountains Trail Map, White Mountains Hiking; USGS: Mount Carrigain, Stairs Mountain; Wilderness Maps: Crawford Notch; State Park map.

Stairs Mountain 3,463'

Stairs Mountain lies farther out on **Davis Path** than Mount Crawford (previous description)—about four and a half miles from the trailhead. From the parking area, cross the river on a suspension bridge, and after a mile of easy walking you reach the old bridle path (constructed about 150 years ago) which soon commences to switchback up the southwest flank of Mt. Crawford. At 2.2 miles, a side path heads left to the open summit of Crawford where there are outstanding views of the classic glacial valley of Crawford Notch. Continuing on Davis Path, at 3.7 miles the Parker Trail (leads to Parker Mtn. and Bartlett) enters from the right. At 4 miles, you reach **Stairs Col** at the base of **Giant Stairs** (see photo), and after a steep zigzagging climb, you finally attain the summit of Stairs Mountain at 4.4 miles. Take the side trail right 0.2 mile to the clifftop viewpoint and enjoy the reward for your efforts.

6 hours and 9.2 miles roundtrip. Elevation gain: 2,500'
Approach: Drive west on US Route 302 from Bartlett for six miles to the Notchland Inn. Trailhead parking is on the right, just off the highway.

Mount Isolation 4,004'

Mount Isolation, the most remote of New Hampshire's 4,000' peaks, is also traversed by **Davis Path**. Start out as for Crawford and Stairs (above) and continue past Stairs Mountain (4.4 miles), reaching **Mount Davis** (3,819') at 8.5 miles (a spur path leads to the summit and a good view). Finally at 9.7 miles, you reach the side path to the summit of Mount Isolation with its sweeping, panoramic views. Return by the same route or one of several alternates—we mention two of them. 1) From the summit continue north (3.3 miles) on Davis Path to Boott Spur, turn right and descend Boott Spur Trail to Tuckerman Ravine Trail and Pinkham Notch. 2) Another route is to continue north only 1.2 miles on Davis Path to Isolation Trail; here head left and descend to Dry River and follow Dry River Trail about 5 miles back to Route 302.

8-14 hours, 19.4 miles, elevation gain: over 3,000' (up and down Davis Path)

Stairs Mountain on the Davis Path

Robert Kozlow

11 Franconia Notch

Franconia Notch is a beautiful glacial valley, blessed with waterfalls, lakes, soaring mountainsides, and towering cliffs. It is perhaps the most dramatic of all the White Mountain notches. Home of New Hampshire's landmark Old Man of the Mountain and other famous natural features, as well as Cannon Mountain Ski Area, the Notch is a mecca for hikers, skiers, and climbers—it is a busy place winter and summer. The spectacular and immensely popular traverse of Franconia Ridge is one of the finest hikes in the eastern United States—many would say the finest. Near the southern end of the chain of high peaks, Franconia Notch is the starting point for hut to hut trips north along the Appalachian Trail to Galehead, Zealand, Lakes of the Clouds, over Mount Washington, across the high ridge of the Northern Presidentials and down to Pinkham Notch.

Franconia Ridge and Mount Lafayette (5,260')

This steep ridge, scarred by rock slides, towers 3,000' over I-93 in Franconia Notch. It provides some of the most alpine hiking in the eastern U.S., and includes four of NH's 4,000-footers. The **Appalachian Trail** traverses the highest part of the ridge, and eight trails access it. The classic route is as follows: From Lafayette Place, ascend the **Falling Waters Trail**. The trail winds up alongside a stream, crossing and recrossing it, and passes small waterfalls. As the trail swings up the steep mountainside, it travels through a spruce–balsam forest in its upper section before reaching treeline just below **Little Haystack** at 3.2 miles and 4,760'. Continue north (left) from here along the barren ridgecrest on **Franconia Ridge Trail**, passing over **Mt. Lincoln** (5,089') after 3.9 miles and finally reaching the summit of **Mt. Lafayette** at 4.8 miles. The ridge is high and narrow (but not precariously so), with long, very steep slopes on either side, especially on the west. The wide views down into Franconia Notch and the Pemigewasset Basin are stunning, but with this openness comes exposure to the elements. It is entirely out in the open, except for some scrubby growth south of

From Mt. Lafayette south along Franconia Ridge   Dick Smith

Lafayette's summit. Careful with the weather here! From the top
of Lafayette, cairns mark **Greenleaf Trail**, as it heads left (west) off
the summit down steep, rocky slopes to **Greenleaf Hut**. To return
to Lafayette Place, follow **Old Bridle Path** down the steep, inter-
mittently open ridge with dramatic views into Walker Ravine;
Franconia Ridge looms high overhead. The hike is done in either
direction. Because of its accessibility and appeal, it is also extremely popular—there are hikers on the traverse most days of the year.

   7 hours, 9 miles, elevation gain: 3,850'
   Approach: *Lafayette Place is eight miles north of I-93 exit 32 (Lincoln).*
   There are parking areas on both sides of the parkway.

Greenleaf Hut is a fine destination in its own right. Follow the **Old
Bridle Path** (or Greenleaf Trail, see next page) for 2.9 miles from
Lafayette Place. Operated by the AMC, it is a full-service hut offering meals and bunks during the summer and fall. Contact the AMC
for reservations. Allow about 2½ hours up and 1½ hours down.

Mount Lafayette via Greenleaf Trail

The panoramic view from Lafayette is exceptional: nearby Cannon Cliff and Lonesome Lake to the west, the Pemigewasset Basin to the east and, spread out in all directions, most of NH's high mountains. Take the Greenleaf Trail, climbing moderately, skirting the base of the impressive cliffs opposite the "Old Man," reaching narrow, rocky **Eagle Pass** at 1.5 miles. From here the trail climbs steeply, coming into the open just below beautifully situated **Greenleaf Hut**, at 2.7 miles and over 2,000' above your starting point. Pass through the last scrubby trees and make the final 1,050' climb up Lafayette's windswept summit cone. Descend by the same route.

6 hours, 7.6 miles, elevation gain: 3,300'

Approach: Park at the Cannon Ski Area Tramway. Walk through the underpass and turn left for the trailhead.

Mount Lafayette via Skookumchuck Trail

This moderately graded trail climbs 4.2 miles to Franconia Ridge where it ends on the **Garfield Ridge Trail** (the AT), 0.8 mile north of Mount Lafayette. In good weather, the final section up Lafayette is a beautiful 30-minute walk above treeline across Lafayette's North Peak. Descend same the trail or via **Greenleaf Trail**.

7 hours, 10 miles, elevation gain: 3,330'

Approach: Approaching from the south, take I-93 exit 35 and proceed north on US 3 0.7 mile to the parking lot on the right.

Artist's Bluff (2,368') and Bald Mountain

This is the classic short hike of the area. The view from Artist's Bluff of Cannon Mountain and Franconia Notch is one of the better-known images of New Hampshire. Some hikers do a 1.6-mile loop hike using the two trailheads on Route 18, but the shorter version is to hike up and down steep and rocky Artist's Bluff. Use the lower trailhead for this alternative.

1¼ hours, 1.6 miles (loop), elevation gain: 400'

Approach: At Exit 3 on the parkway, take Route 18 for 0.2 mile to Artist's Bluff trailhead, or 0.4 mile farther to the lot across from Peabody Lodge.

Cannon Cliff

Richard Bailey

Natural Features in Franconia Notch

The natural features in Franconia Notch have been tourist attractions for many years. In fact, when Thomas Jefferson was president, his likeness with the **Old Man of the Mountain** was noted. This most famous natural feature in New Hampshire —it is the state symbol—is a 40'-high cluster of rocks precariously attached high on the cliffs of **Cannon Mountain**. The face can be seen from **Profile Lake**, just south of the tramway at the Cannon Mountain Ski Area. **The Flume** is the name given to a trench-like 800'-long gorge in Flume Brook, fed by a gushing waterfall (Avalanche Falls) at its upper end. A system of boardwalks allows for close-up viewing. (Admission is charged.) **The Basin** is an interesting, 30-foot wide pothole, scoured out of beautiful, smooth granite by the Pemigewasset River. It is reached by an easy walk. The State of New Hampshire, which administers Franconia Notch State Park, supplies an excellent little topo map, free of charge.

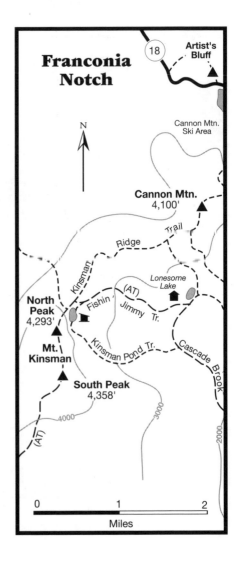

Franconia Notch

18

Artist's Bluff

Cannon Mtn. Ski Area

N

Cannon Mtn.
4,100'

Ridge   Trail

Kinsman

Lonesome Lake

(AT)

Fishin'   Jimmy   Tr.

North Peak
4,293'

Kinsman Pond Tr.

Cascade Brook

Mt. Kinsman

South Peak
4,358'

4000

3000

2000

(AT)

| 0 | 1 | 2 |

Miles

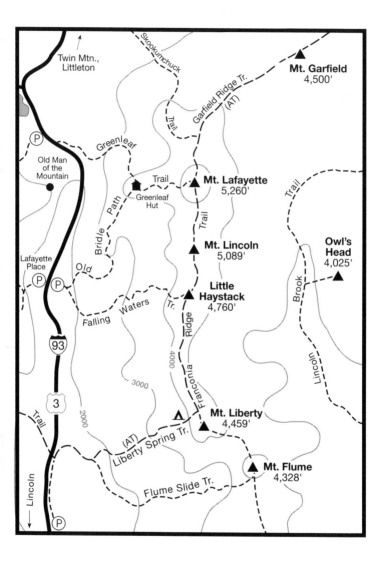

Cannon Mountain 4,100'

With a major alpine ski area, an aerial tramway that operates all summer, and an observation deck on the summit, Cannon is one of our more developed peaks. If solitude is what you are looking for, you might want to look elsewhere. The hiking route, the **Kinsman Ridge Trail**, though steep, is tame by comparison to the dozens of rock climbing routes on Cannon's 1,000' east face. The trail switchbacks to a superb view at 1.5 miles (on an unmarked side path left). The trail continues, steep and rough; the footing worsens as you climb. At two miles, bear left on the **Rim Trail**. Continue for 0.2 mile and turn right on a gravel path to the summit and observation platform. Descend by the same trail.

5½ hours, 4.4 miles, elevation gain: 2,100'

Approach: Take I-93 to Cannon Mountain Ski Area in Franconia Notch. In the tramway parking area, stay left and follow the AMC signs.

Lonesome Lake

The climb to Lonesome Lake is very popular. Since it's only 1.5 miles to the lake and 0.2 mile on to **Lonesome Lake Hut**, this trip is a particular favorite with families. Although not without a fair amount of climbing (1,000'), the lake and the hut seem to be adequate reward. The views across the valley are great, especially late in the fall. An 0.8-mile loop trail (soggy along the west side) traces the shoreline, giving clear views over to Franconia Ridge. Descend the same way you came up, by the **Lonesome Lake Trail**. For those who want to climb **Cannon Mountain**, continue on Lonesome Lake Trail, ending at **Kinsman Ridge Trail** after one mile. Here, bear right and continue over steep, rather difficult terrain to the summit (2 miles from the lake), with its observation deck. Return by the same route.

2½ hours, 3.4 miles, elevation gain: 1,000' (Lonesome Lake)

Approach: Park at Lafayette Place, two miles south of Cannon Mountain Ski Area. There are parking lots on both sides of the parkway.

Mount Flume from Mount Liberty   Matthew Cull

North Kinsman and South Kinsman (4,358')

This is a demanding and rewarding hike with spectacular views of the Franconia Range. From Lafayette Place, climb up to **Lonesome Lake Hut**. Continue on **Fishin' Jimmy Trail** (the AT south) and, after some long, steep sections, pass the spur trail (left) to **Kinsman Pond** and its shelter (worth the slight detour). Continue to the **Kinsman Ridge Trail** and head left to reach **North Kinsman Peak** (4,293'), four miles from the road. There is a dramatic lookout ledge just east of the main trail. Continue for a mile to the higher South Kinsman Peak with its two bald summit areas. The few small trees do not seriously obscure the view. Moosilauke looms impressively to the south, and to the east, Franconia Ridge dominates the horizon. Return the way you came. The AT continues south to Kinsman Notch and Moosilauke.

7–8 hours, 10.4 miles, total elevation gain: 3,400'

Approach: Park at Lafayette Place on I-93 (parkway), eight miles north of North Lincoln. Kinsman is on the west side of the highway.

Mount Pemigewasset 2,557'

Also known as **Indian Head**, Mount Pemigewasset is a moderate climb offering great views from a ledgy summit. From the Flume parking area, follow signs for the **Mount Pemigewasset Trail**. It passes under the highway and climbs moderate slopes, reaching a dramatic cliff's edge after 1.8 miles. The edge is abrupt, so be careful here. The views are excellent, especially of nearby Franconia Ridge. Return by the same route.

2 hours, 3.6 miles round trip, elevation gain: 1150'

Approach: Park at the north end of the Flume Gorge parking area. The trail runs along the bike path for the first 150 yards.

Mt. Flume (4,328') and Mt. Liberty (4,459')

Flume and Liberty are the lower pair of the four main summits of Franconia Ridge, and they can be done as a long loop hike. The mostly wooded traverse between the two is less of an alpine experience than Franconia Ridge, but the **Flume Slide Trail** is one of the hardest trails in the state. From the Flume hiker parking area, take the **White House Trail** 0.9 mile to **Liberty Spring Trail**, turn right and follow it for 0.6 mile before branching right onto the Flume Slide Trail. It climbs quite moderately for about 2.5 miles, crossing and recrossing several streams. The next half mile or so ascends a brutally steep chute-like gash in the heavily forested mountainside, up smooth and at times wet rocks—a very prolonged, strenuous climb. At 4.7 miles from the start you reach the ridge. Head left 0.1 mile on the Osseo Trail to the top of **Mt. Flume**, where (hopefully) the panoramic views will make it all worthwhile! Continue north on **Franconia Ridge Trail** to the summit of Mt. Liberty, 1.2 miles farther. Again, there are excellent views of Franconia Ridge, the Pemigewasset Wilderness, and many summits. Continue, descending north for 0.3 mile to **Liberty Spring Trail**. Turn left and descend steeply, passing the tent site after 0.3 mile and reaching the White House Trail after 2.9 miles.

8 hours, 10 miles, elevation gain: 3,700'

Approach: Take Exit 1 off the Franconia Notch parkway (I-93) and proceed to the Flume hiker parking, 0.2 mile north of the Flume entrance.

Mount Garfield 4,500'

Garfield's isolated, rocky summit offers a unique vantage point. To the east the Bonds and the Twin Range are higher, while nearby Franconia Ridge and Mt. Lafayette block the horizon to the west; yet to the north and to the south the landscape drops away dramatically. For the first few miles the **Garfield Trail** climbs gently through a mixed forest, but it steepens just before reaching the **Garfield Ridge Trail** (AT) at 4.8 miles. Here, head right, and climb abruptly up to the rocky, open summit with its old stone foundation (good protection from wind) at 5 miles. Descend the same way. When seen from nearby ridges—the Bonds or Franconia Ridge, for example—Mt. Garfield's bulky mass is easy to identify.

6½ hours, 10 miles, elevation gain: 3,100'

Approach: *From Franconia Notch, drive 6 miles north on US 3, turn right on Gale River Loop Road; the trailhead parking is in to the left at 1.2 miles.*

Franconia Notch to Zealand Hut (3 days)

The hike from Lafayette Place in Franconia Notch to Zealand Road, near Crawford Notch, is a rugged and spectacular 21-mile traverse. Three AMC huts and several campsites provide stopping points. A popular itinerary is as follows: Hike up to **Greenleaf Hut** the first afternoon, continuing over Mts. Lafayette and Garfield to **Galehead Hut** the next day. On day three, make the steep climb up South Twin (4,902'). Continue across the alpine slopes of Mt. Guyot on Twinway, past spectacular Zeacliff, and on down to **Zealand Falls Hut**. Garfield Ridge has campsites 0.4 mile east of Garfield summit, and there are tentsites and an open shelter 0.2 mile east off Bondcliff Trail, 0.6 mile south from Twinway.

From Lafayette Place in Franconia Notch to Zealand Road:

US Route 3 to Greenleaf Hut: . . . . . . *2.9 miles.*
Greenleaf Hut to Galehead Hut: . . . . *7.7 miles.*
Galehead Hut to Zealand Falls Hut: . . . *7 miles.*
Zealand Falls Hut to Zealand Road: . . *2.7 miles.*

Maps: *DeLorme; Map Adventures; Wilderness:* Franconia Notch; *AMC #2* Franconia - Pemigewasset; *USGS: Franconia, Lincoln, South Twin.*

Campgrounds: *Two in the Park; see also info for Chapters 9 and 12.*

12 Kancamagus Highway

Stretching 32 miles east from Lincoln to Conway, the "Kanc" runs through one of the largest undeveloped areas in New Hampshire. A remote and beautiful drive in a vast forest, the highway is bounded on the north by the Pemigewasset Wilderness and on the south by the Sandwich Range and the surprisingly wild–looking Osceola peaks. The views are superb, especially from the road's high point, Kancamagus Pass (2,855'). Proceeding from west to east we give the most popular hikes accessed from the Kancamagus Highway.

Franconia Falls

After crossing the Pemigewasset River on a suspension bridge, the **Lincoln Woods Trail** follows an old railroad bed for 2.8 miles. Here a short side trail (15 min.) leads left to the cascades and sculpted granite of Franconia Falls. This is a popular hike over very easy ground to some fun swimming holes. A permit (free) is required to visit the falls; a limit of 60 visitors at one time is currently in effect. Check in with the Forest Service ranger before hiking.

2½ hours, 6.4 miles, total climb: 210'

Approach: From I-93 at Lincoln, drive east five miles on the Kancamagus Highway to Lincoln Woods parking area. The Forest Service information center is staffed during busy periods.

Mount Bond 4,698'

Although the goal of this hike is Mt. Bond, the highest of "the Bonds", the steep, dynamic views from **Bondcliff** are the real high point. From Bondcliff you peer straight into a wild, steep-sided alpine valley, while the trail ahead traces the narrow ridgeline to the open summit of Mount Bond, 1.2 miles distant. To reach Bondcliff, follow the **Lincoln Woods Trail** to Franconia Brook, cross the river on a bridge and continue east (still on very easy terrain) on the **Wilderness Trail**, reaching the Camp 16 clearing after 4.7 miles, about 2½ hours from the car. The **Bondcliff Trail** heads north (left), climbing moderately (there is a scramble near the top),

Franconia Falls
Robert Kozlow

reaching the clifftop summit of **Bondcliff** (4,265') after another 4.4 miles and 3 hours. From here, continue along the spectacular, exposed mile-long ridge to the summit of Mount Bond, over 10 miles from the highway. Be careful on this open section in stormy conditions or with poor visibility. Return by the same route. For very strong hikers the entire trip is manageable as a long day, but most will choose to camp along the way. A campsite is located 2.7 miles up the East Branch Road—check with the Forest Service for current camping regulations. **West Bond**, at 4,540' NH's 17th highest peak, is reached by continuing north from Mt. Bond's summit for 0.6 mile to **West Bond Spur**. Head left on the spur for a half mile to the summit, with its exciting views of Bondcliff and the Pemi Wilderness. (Page 5 has a photo of Bondcliff and West Bond.)

One or two days, 20 miles, elevation gain: 3,800'
Approach: From I-93 at Lincoln, drive east five miles on the Kancamagus Highway to the Lincoln Woods parking area.

Complete Traverse of the Bonds: Hiking through to the Zealand area and Route 302 (Crawford Notch) is a standard continuation of the above trip. From **Mount Bond** it is 1.3 miles on Bondcliff Trail to **Twinway** (AT). The Guyot tent site and shelter is a good place to spend the night, and is reached by a 0.2-mile side trail which branches right off Bondcliff Trail 0.7 mile beyond Mount Bond. Upon reaching Twinway, bear right, cross the summit of **Mount Guyot** (4,580') and, after a short descent, traverse up across **Zealand Mountain** (4,260'), where a very short spur trail leads left to the viewless summit. About 1.3 miles before reaching Zealand Falls Hut, you will pass the spur trail (right) to Zeacliff's famous view across Zealand Notch to Mt. Carrigain. **Zealand Falls Hut** is 3–4 hours (5.5 miles) from Mount Bond, and Zealand Road is another hour and a half (2.7 miles). See **Crawford Notch** (Chapter 9) for approaching the Bonds from the Zealand side. Almost the entire stretch from the Twinway–Bondcliff Trail intersection to Bondcliff's summit is out in the open or at treeline. This, combined with remoteness and wild mountain views, makes Bondcliff Trail one of the most exciting trails in the Northeast.

Owl's Head Mountain 4,025'

Peakbaggers' nemesis! Why climb this undistinguished mound in the middle of the Pemi Wilderness? Because it's there and because it's over 1,219 meters high. To reach this very remote 4,000'-footer take **Lincoln Woods Trail** (described previously) and continue on **Franconia Brook Trail**, reaching **Lincoln Brook Trail** at 4.6 miles. Now branch left, and after crossing first the Franconia branch of the Pemigewasset River and then the Lincoln Brook branch, the trail parallels Lincoln Brook for 3.3 miles, where it reaches a landslide descending from Owl's Head; watch for the cairn. Ascend the slide and follow the unmaintained trail through dense woods to the summit. There are good views from the slide but none from the summit, unless you climb a tree. Return by the same route. Well done!

9–10 hours, 18 miles, total climb: 2,950'
Approach: Park at Lincoln Woods on the Kancamagus Highway.

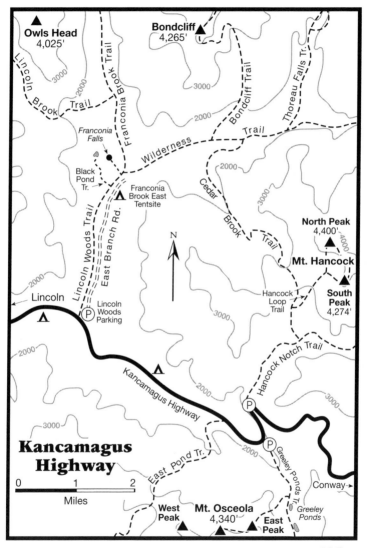

Mount Hancock, North and South Peaks

Although probably hiked mostly by peakbaggers working on their list of 4,000'-footers, this is a fun trip offering a sharp contrast between easy walking and very steep climbing. From the trailhead, take the **Hancock Notch Trail** over very easy ground for 1.7 miles, then head left on the **Cedar Brook Trail** for 0.7 mile, where the **Hancock Loop Trail** branches right. The 4.6-mile loop over North (4,400') and South Peak (4,274') is much rougher, and is as steep as the approach is gentle. At the "loop junction" the trail to North Peak plunges down to a stream crossing before beginning its steep and merciless climb, slackening just before the somewhat indistinct summit. Follow the side trail left for great views of Osceola and nearby Carrigain. To complete the loop, continue over relatively easy ground to South Peak (where there are good views east and north through the trees) before dropping very steeply back down to the loop junction. Return to the Kancamagus Highway the way you came.

6¼ hours, 9.4 miles, total climb: 1,780'

Approach: *Drive east from Lincoln on the Kancamagus Highway for 10 miles to the Hancock Notch Trail, located on the left just past the Greeley Ponds Trail. Parking is just around the bend on the right.*

Greeley Ponds

An easy trail (yellow-blazed) leads to these two small ponds in **Mad River Notch**, with the East Peak of Osceola soaring overhead. From the Kancamagus Highway, the upper pond is reached after 1.4 miles and **Lower Greeley Pond** at 1.9 miles. Because of the high use it receives, camping in the vicinity of the ponds (the Greeley Ponds Scenic Area) is not permitted. From the lower pond, the Greeley Pond Trail continues over gentle terrain down to Waterville Valley, 3 miles distant. See chapter 14 for the approach from Waterville Valley; refer to the Backcountry Skiing chapter for the ski touring version of this trip.

2½ hours, 4 miles, total climb: 450' (to Lower Greeley Pond)

Approach: *The trailhead is 9.5 miles east of Lincoln on the right (south) side of the Kancamagus Highway.*

Sabbaday Falls

Only 15 minutes from the highway, interesting water chutes and basins scoured out of smooth granite await you. The **Sabbaday Brook Trail** runs south—the clearly marked trailhead is 15.5 miles west of NH 16, on the south side of the highway. Watch for signs for the falls on the left after you've walked about 10 minutes.

Sabbaday Falls

Robert Kozlow

East Peak of Osceola 4,156'

The **Mount Osceola Trail** branches right off the **Greeley Ponds Trail** after 1.2 miles, about 30 minutes from the Kancamagus Highway. (Upper Greeley Pond is just beyond this trail junction.) The trail quickly begins its long and at times quite steep climb to the summit of Osceola's East Peak. After traversing beneath some high cliffs, the trail ascends gullies and crosses slides, reaching the summit 1.5 miles from the Greeley Ponds Trail.

4 hours, 5.6 miles, climb: 2,250'

Approach: *Use the trailhead for Greeley Ponds, 9.5 miles east of Lincoln on the Kancamagus Highway.*

Mt. Chocorua (3,475') via Champney Falls Trail

A moderate climb makes this a relatively easy and popular route up Chocorua. Only the Champney Falls Trail approaches this famous mountain from the north. The first 2 miles climb gentle grades with the final half mile switchbacking more steeply up to the ridge. At this point, about 2½ hours and 3 miles from the car, the Middle Sister Trail branches off to the left and very soon thereafter the Champney Falls Trail ends at the Piper Trail. Continue for 0.6 mile (right) on the **Piper Trail**, soon coming out onto open rock, reaching the summit about 3 hours (3.8 miles) from the road. There are great views in all directions, of Washington, Carrigain, the Sandwich Range, Osceola, and others. Descend by the same route. During periods of heavy runoff, **Champney Falls** is worth the short side trip. The marked side trail branches left about 1.4 miles from the trailhead. Please bear in mind that Mount Chocorua is extremely popular and tends to be quite crowded on good weather days.

5 hours, 7.6 miles, total climb: 2,250'

Approach: The trailhead is about 20 miles east of Lincoln on the south side of the Kancamagus Highway.

Mount Potash 2,660'

A fun, short hike to great views of the Swift River Valley, Potash is understandably popular with families. Across from Passaconaway Campground the yellow-blazed **Mount Potash Trail** coincides with **Downes Brook Trail**, soon branching to the right, after crossing Downes Brook. It climbs moderately and finishes with an enjoyable section up across open ledges (exercise care, especially if the rock is wet) with panoramic views of surrounding mountains.

3 hours, 4.4 miles, total climb: 1,390'

Approach: The trailhead for Mt. Potash is on the south side of the Kancamagus Highway, 13.5 miles west of Conway and NH 16.

Maps: Wilderness Map Co.: *Kancamagus Highway;* Delorme; *AMC #3 Crawford Notch-Sandwich Range;* USGS: *Mt. Osceola, South Twin Mtn., Mt. Chocorua;* Forest Service; Wonalancet Out Door Club.

White Mountain National Forest

Most of the hiking in this guide book is in the White Mountain National Forest (WMNF), a huge, undeveloped area of woods, lakes, and mountains that spreads across northern New Hampshire and into western Maine. Administered by the U.S. Forest Service, the more or less contiguous 770,000 acres is actively managed for camping, hiking, fishing, cross country skiing, snowmobiling, logging, wildlife habitat, and watershed protection. There are five federally-designated wilderness areas within the WMNF: Great Gulf, Presidential Range-Dry River, Sandwich Range, Caribou-Speckled Mountain and Pemigewasset. Wilderness areas are more protected, and hence more restricted than non-wilderness areas.

The 1,200 miles of hiking trails in the National Forest are maintained by the Forest Service with considerable help from the AMC and other hiking organizations. Forest Service Visitor Centers in Gorham, Conway, Bethel (Maine), Bethlehem, Plymouth, and the Supervisor's Office in Laconia provide up-to-date information on hiking trails, camping and ski routes. A good selection of maps and guide books is available as well as free, informative trip sheets for suggested outings.

The Forest Service has implemented a parking permit fee for recreational users of the WMNF. The permit fees, $3 for one-time use, $5 for a week, and $20 for a year's use, apply to all unattended vehicles parked in Forest Service maintained parking areas. Permits can be purchased at many locations throughout the region. Visitors passing through the area and only temporarily parked are exempted.

Camping: There are six Forest Service campgrounds along the Kancamagus Highway. Hancock and Big Rock Campgrounds are near Lincoln Woods. Farther to the east, Passaconaway and Jigger Johnson are near the trails for Mt. Potash and Mt. Chocorua (Champney Falls Trail). Private campgrounds in Conway and Woodstock.

13 | Mt. Chocorua and the Eastern Sandwich Range

Mount Chocorua (3,475') is one of the most-photographed mountains in New England, and its rocky spire is one of the most popular hiking destinations in the state. Three routes are given here, and a fourth route, via Champney Falls Trail, is described in the Kancamagus chapter. The views from Chocorua's summit are superb: to the north, Mt. Washington reigns over the Presidentials, and to the west, in the Sandwich Range Wilderness, the companion peaks of Whiteface Mountain (4,020') and Mount Passaconaway (4,043') dominate. The Wonalancet Out Door Club maintains an excellent network of trails in the Sandwich Range Wilderness, where the spectacular Blueberry Ledge Trail on Whiteface Mountain is probably the outstanding hike.

Mount Chocorua from the east: Piper Trail

This popular and accessible trail starts out following an old logging road over easy terrain. Soon after crossing into the National Forest, the Weetamoo Trail branches left (at 0.8 mile), and at 1.4 miles the Nickerson Ledge Trail leads off to the right. After climbing past a view towards Carter Ledge the trail steepens and climbs in a switchbacking fashion, reaching the steep spur trail (0.2 mile) up to Camp Penacook shelter at 3.1 miles. Glimpses of the rocky summit soaring high overhead are a little daunting. Now mostly on exposed bedrock, the trail leads steeply up to the summit ridge. Continue along the ridge, climbing on ledges to reach the top, 4.5 miles from your starting point. After taking in the views, descend by the same route. This is a long, interesting hike on an enjoyable and well laid out path.

> *6-7 hours, 9 miles, total climb: 2,800'*
> *Approach: The trailhead is on NH 16, 6.5 miles south of Conway, at the Davies Campground and General Store. The trailhead is located in the White Mountain Nat. Forest, thus the Forest Service usage fee applies.*

Mount Chocorua   Ned Therrien

Mount Chocorua via Middle Sister

From the campground start out on the **Carter Ledge Trail**, but branch right onto **Middle Sister Trail** after one mile and continue climbing, reaching a little col on the Three Sisters Ridge at about 3.5 miles. In another half mile the Carter Ledge Trail re-enters from the left as the Middle Sister Trail continues its rocky traverse across Middle and First Sister. At 3,330' Middle Sister is almost as high as Chocorua. The **Champney Falls Trail** joins from the right at 5.1 miles. Continue on the **Piper Trail**, staying left to complete the remaining 0.6 mile to the top. For such a pointed mountain, Chocorua's summit area is surprisingly spread out. On the descent, backtrack to Carter Ledge Trail and follow it (3.7 miles) to the campground, passing popular **Carter Ledge** (good viewpoint) about a mile below the ridge.

8 hours, 9.5 miles, total climb: about 3,000'

Approach: Start from the White Ledge Campground on the west side of NH 16, 5.5 miles south of Conway.

The Brook Trail and Liberty Trail Loop

Since both trails start at the end of Paugus Mill Road and rejoin just below the summit, and since one is a bit steep and the other rather easy, together they make a great loop trip. From the parking area ascend the steeper Brook Trail by continuing (past the gate) on **Paugus Mill Road** for 0.1 mile, where the actual trail branches right. Climbing at times alongside a small brook, the trail passes a small waterfall at two miles and comes out onto open, somewhat steep ledges at about three miles, where there are good views south to the lakes. On the ledges the trail is marked with yellow paint and cairns. At 3.4 miles the Liberty Trail merges from the right, and it is a fun scramble up to the wide-open summit, which is completely exposed to the elements! On the descent, stay left at the intersection 0.2 mile below the summit to pick up the Liberty Trail. After passing **Jim Liberty Cabin** and descending switchbacks, the gradient gradually slackens as this former bridle path brings you gently back to your starting point. The descent via Liberty Trail is 3.9 miles. Although it is a less varied option, simply ascending and descending Liberty Trail is very popular. The Liberty Trail is one of the easiest routes up the mountain.

6 hours, 7.1 miles, total climb: 2,550' (loop)

Approach: From NH 113A, three miles east of Wonalancet (or six miles west of the village of Chocorua), take Fowler's Mill Road (Forest Road 68) north 1.2 miles, turn left on Paugus Mill Road, and continue 0.8 mile to the gate and parking.

Wonalancet Out Door Club

The Wonalancet Out Door Club (WODC) does an excellent job of maintaining and signing trails in the area. The club publishes the *Trail Map and Guide to the Sandwich Range Wilderness* (1995). Coverage includes the eastern portion of Waterville Valley, Whiteface, Passaconaway, and the western slopes of Chocorua.

Camping: There are six Forest Service campgrounds along the Kancamagus Highway and another, White Ledge Campground, is on NH 16, 5.5 miles south of Conway. White Lake State Park is in Tamworth.

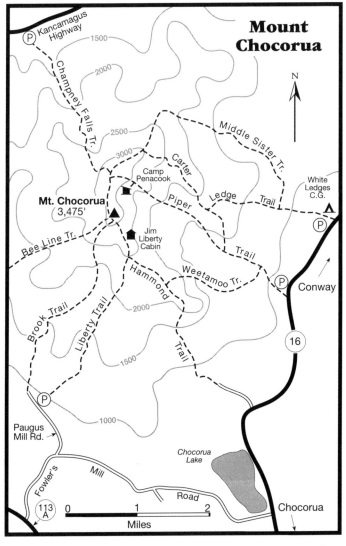

Mount Chocorua

Kancamagus Highway

Champney Falls Tr.

1500

2000

2500

3000

Middle Sister Tr.

N

Carter

Camp
Penacook

Mt. Chocorua
3,475'

Piper

Ledge

Trail

White
Ledges
C.G.

P

Bee Line Tr.

Jim
Liberty
Cabin

Trail

Hammond

Weetamoo Tr.

P

Conway

Brook Trail

Liberty Trail

2000

16

1500

Trail

P

1000

Paugus
Mill Rd.

Fowler's

Mill

Road

Chocorua
Lake

113
A

0   1   2

Miles

Chocorua

Mt. Whiteface and Mt. Passaconaway (4,043')

The **Blueberry Ledge Trail** offers an exciting and challenging route up the south side of Mt. Whiteface (4,020'). The loop hike including Passaconaway rates as one of the classics. Walk up Ferncroft Road and, following signs, cross the river and pick up the trail. It climbs gently to moderately and reaches an open area (good views south) at 1.6 miles, where the Blueberry Ledge Cutoff rejoins from the right. The trail is steeper from here onward, but is always varied and enjoyable. After passing a fine lookout with a view into the high basin between Passaconaway and Whiteface, the trail ascends a very narrow, steep ridge. The exciting finale up slabs and ramps ends at a spectacular viewpoint just below the south summit. Continue across the wooded main summit on **Rollins Trail** and make the traverse over to Passaconaway (involves a descent of 800') reaching **Dicey's Mill Trail** after 2 miles of somewhat rough up and down travel. Head left up Dicey's Mill Trail for 0.9 mile to the top. After locating the viewpoint just beyond the summit, return on Dicey's Mill Trail all the way back to Ferncroft Road, a distance of 4.3 miles. Dicey's Mill Trail is the standard ascent route for Mt. Passaconaway from Ferncroft.

8 hours, 11.8 miles, total climb: 3,800'
Approach: From Center Sandwich, follow NH 113 and 113A north 10.7 miles to Wonalancet. Turn left on Ferncroft Road; the hiker parking area is 0.5 mile in on the right.

Mount Wonalancet 2,800'

Wonalancet is the prominent, rounded peak just above Ferncroft Road. From the parking area take **Old Mast Road** (hiking trail) to "Four-Way" (at 2 miles) and head left on **Walden Trail**, ascending the "Hedgehog" and passing several viewpoints. At 0.9 mile bear left on **Wonalancet Range Trail** and traverse **Hibbard Mtn.** (2,910') to Mt. Wonalancet. There are good outlooks near the top of Hibbard and below Wonalancet's wooded summit. It is 1.8 miles down to the Ferncroft parking area from Wonalancet's crest.

4.5 hours, 6.2 miles, total climb: 2,300' (loop hike)
Approach: As above, from the Ferncroft Road trailhead.

Maps: WODC; AMC: #3 *Crawford Notch-Sandwich Range*; Map Adventures; USGS: *Mt Chocorua, Silver Lake, Mount Tripyramid.*

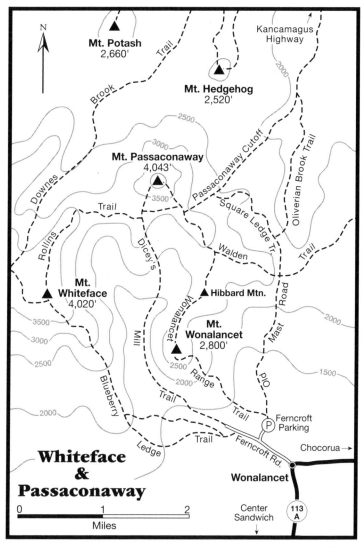

N

Mt. Potash
2,660'

Kancamagus
Highway

Brook

Trail

Mt. Hedgehog
2,520'

2000

2500

Downes

3000

Mt. Passaconaway
4,043'

Passaconaway Cutoff

Trail

3500

Square Ledge Tr.

Oliverian Brook Trail

Rollins

Dicey's

Walden

Mt. Whiteface
4,020'

Hibbard Mtn.

Road

Mast

Trail

3500

3000

Mill

Mt. Wonalancet
2,800'

Wonalancet

2000

2500

Range

Old

2500

Blueberry

2000

Trail

Trail

1500

Ledge

Trail

Ferncroft
Parking

P

**Whiteface
&
Passaconaway**

Ferncroft Rd.

Chocorua →

Wonalancet

0   1   2

Miles

Center
Sandwich

113
A

↓

14 Waterville Valley

This major summer and winter resort area is the starting point for several excellent hikes. Five of New Hampshire's 4,000-footers are here, including North Tripyramid with its difficult slide route. Mount Osceola is the dominant peak, while Mount Tecumseh—the skiers' mountain—offers an easy ascent. The exciting loop hike over nearby Welch and Dickey gives great views for relatively little effort. For nordic skiers, Livermore Road and Greeley Ponds Trail are excellent backcountry trips. Waterville Valley is nestled in a mountain basin at the end of NH 49, 11 miles north of I-93's Campton exit. The village spreads across the open valley floor, and high mountains crowd around on all sides. The highway enters through the narrow cut formed by the Mad River.

Mount Tripyramid   4,180'

This steep and remote mountain, with slides on its north and south peaks, offers a challenging 11-mile loop. In fact it is one of the most difficult hikes in the state. From the parking area, walk 3.6 miles up **Livermore Road** (a beautifully maintained woods road) to the **North Slide Trail**. After a short passage through dense woods you arrive at the base of the imposing North Slide. Take your time climbing up the slabs and enjoy the view! If wet or icy, this route is not advised. Under normal, dry conditions, it takes about 30 minutes to ascend the slide. Exiting left at the top of the slabs you reach the summit of **North Peak**, with its somewhat obscured views. Continue along the narrow and heavily wooded ridge to **Middle Peak** (4,140') and on to **South Peak** (4,090'). From here descend the **South Slide**. (Stay right at the junction with the Sleeper Trail.) The loose rock and scree of South Slide may be a little disconcerting, but it is easier and safer than the North Slide's relatively smooth slab. At the base of the slide, stay on **South Slide Trail** to Livermore Road, then stroll back to the parking lot.

7 hours, 11 miles, total climb: 2,900'

Approach: *Follow signs from the resort and, after crossing the river, the Livermore Road trailhead is on the right.*

North Tripyramid on the left, South Tripyramid on the right   James Bond

Easier route up North Tripyramid: If conditions advise against tackling the North Slide, use the **Scaur Ridge Trail**, located just 0.2 mile farther up **Livermore Road**. It provides an easier and safer route to the top. After 1.2 miles, the Scaur Ridge Trail merges with the **Pine Bend Brook Trail**; turn right onto it, reaching the summit after a final steep section, two miles from Livermore Road.

There are a number of easier trails on **Snow's Mountain** (3,010'), the site of Waterville Valley's smaller ski area. From the bottom of the chairlift there's a fine 3.3-mile circuit hike affording great views of the village from a couple of outlooks. Another popular family hike, **Cascade Path**, leads past a series of small waterfalls. The Waterville Valley Athletic and Improvement Association (WVAIA) publishes a map with detailed descriptions of these shorter hiking trails.

Mount Osceola 4,340'

Taking its name from Osceola, the Seminole chief, the highest peak in the area forms the northern end of the valley. When facing Tecumseh (the main downhill ski area), it is located to the right and across Tripoli Road. The **Mount Osceola Trail** climbs generally moderate grades to the impressive summit "balcony" at 3.5 miles, where there is a dramatic view of Waterville Valley, Tripyramid, and Osceola's East Peak. The first half of the trail is somewhat rough and rocky, but the upper section offers smoother going.

4½ hours, 7 miles, total climb: 2,070'

Approach: Turn left off NH 49 at the entrance to Waterville Valley onto Tripoli Road. After about five miles, just beyond Thornton Gap, the trailhead parking appears on the right.

East Peak variation: Continuing to East Peak (4,156') adds 2 miles and 900' of climbing to the round trip. From the main summit, drop steeply—one brief section is almost vertical—into a saddle at 3,800' then ascend past a good viewpoint (on the left) to the wooded summit of East Peak, 4.5 miles from Tripoli Road. Return the way you came or see below.

6 hours, 9 miles, total climb: 2,960' (both summits)

The Mount Osceola Trail continues beyond East Peak and makes an extremely steep descent to the **Greeley Ponds Trail** for a total of 5.7 miles from Tripoli Road. To return to Waterville Valley, turn right, walk pass the ponds, and continue on very gentle terrain to the parking area at the foot of Livermore Road.

Mount Tecumseh 4,003'

The lowest of New Hampshire's 4,000-footers, Tecumseh, named for the famed Shawnee chief, is the home of Waterville Valley's alpine ski area. The **Mount Tecumseh Trail** ascends the mountain from the ski area parking lot and continues to a minor summit before dropping down the west side to Tripoli Road. Climbing or descending the mountain by the ski trails is also recommended, since one has a view the entire time—a view that gradually improves with elevation. From the ski area parking lot, follow the Mount Tecumseh Trail up a moderate climb, passing the Sosman Trail at 1.9 miles. (Head south on Sosman 0.2 miles for good views.) Here, follow Mount Tecumseh Trail (right) to the summit. The trail finishes steeply, rewarding you with some partial views of nearby Osceola and, somewhat farther away, the impressive, scarred flank of Tripyramid. Descend by the same route or follow the **Sosman Trail** over to the ski trails.

3½ hours, 4.4 miles, total climb: 2,170'

Approach: Drive up to the ski area (off Tripoli Road). The trail begins across the road from the uppermost parking lot, just below the lodge.

Glacial Action

During the last Ice Age, glaciers advanced and receded numerous times. The last glacial maximum occurred about 20,000 years ago when ice sheets extended as far south as Long Island. The estimated 13,000 feet of constantly moving ice ground away an average of 15 feet of bedrock and, like a river, deposited the material downstream. Chunks of bedrock frozen in moving ice acted like sandpaper grit, scratching the stationary bedrock. Striations, or glacial scratches, are common on nearly all exposed bedrock in New England today, usually in the form of parallel lines on the rock surfaces. While the overall effect of glacial erosion was to smooth the existing topography, many individual features are directly attributed to ice scour. Glaciation had a profound impact on New England's current landscape: deep U-shaped valleys such as Crawford Notch and Franconia Notch, as well as many of our lakes, are the result of glacial scour. Mount Washington's Tuckerman Ravine, a feature known as a cirque, was formed by the erosive action of smaller glaciers left behind by the larger continental glaciers. As the glaciers retreated, they left behind their rock cargo, huge boulders in some cases. These solitary "foreign" rocks are called glacial erratics.

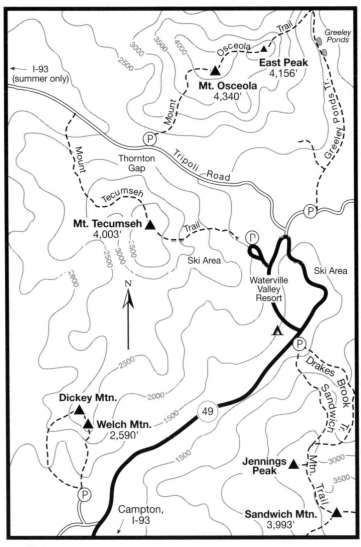

Greeley Ponds

Trail

Osceola

East Peak
4,156'

Mount

Mt. Osceola
4,340'

I-93
(summer only)

Greeley Ponds Tr.

3000

3500

4000

2500

P

Thornton
Gap

Tripoli   Road

Mount

Tecumseh

P

Mt. Tecumseh
4,003'

Trail

Ski Area

N

2500

3000

2500

2500

Waterville
Valley
Resort

Ski Area

P

Drakes Brook

2500

2000

1500

Dickey Mtn.

Welch Mtn.
2,590'

49

Sandwich Tr.

1500

Jennings
Peak

3000

Mtn. Trail

3500

Sandwich

P

Campton,
I-93

Sandwich Mtn.
3,993'

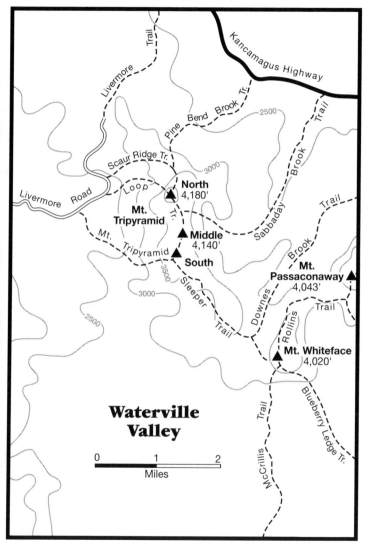

Waterville Valley

Kancamagus Highway

Livermore Trail

Pine Bend Brook Tr.

2500

Scaur Ridge Tr.

3000

Livermore Road

Loop

▲ **North** 4,180'

Mt. Tripyramid

Mt. Tripyramid

Tr.

▲ **Middle** 4,140'

▲ **South**

3500

Sleeper

3000

Trail

2500

Sabbaday Brook Trail

Trail

Brook

Downes

▲ **Mt. Passaconaway** 4,043'

Trail

Rollins

▲ **Mt. Whiteface** 4,020'

Trail

McCrillis

Blueberry Ledge Tr.

0   1   2
Miles

Sandwich Mountain 3,993'

Also known as Sandwich Dome, this mountain offers a solid hike with some excellent views. From NH 49 follow the **Sandwich Mountain Trail** up a generally moderate grade to **Noon Peak**. The trail then runs over gentler terrain, with some viewpoints, to the short side trail to **Jenning's Peak** (3,460'). The views from its rocky summit are the best on the trip! From here the main trail climbs steadily to the wooded summit of Sandwich, with its limited views of Tecumseh and Osceola. The Smarts Brook Trail enters from the right 0.7 mile before the summit. Return the way you came, or branch right on the descent onto **Drakes Brook Trail**, just after the Jenning's Peak spur trail, to make a loop.

Note: The Bennett Street Trail and the Algonquin Trail also leave from the summit area—be sure to take the correct trail.

5½ hours, 7.8 miles, total climb: 2,715'

Approach: The trailhead is on the east side of NH 49, 0.4 mile south of the entrance to Waterville Valley.

Welch (2,605') and Dickey (2,734') Mountains

About half of this varied loop hike is on granite slabs and exposed bedrock—unusual for a low mountain—giving great views of Mad River Valley and the surrounding peaks. From the trailhead stay right and ascend through woods, reaching a large open shoulder about midway up Welch Mtn. From here the trail steepens, threading its way through jack pine and blueberry bushes, at one point ascending a steep, 100-foot slab before reaching the spectacular summit ledges of Welch at two miles. About 20 minutes of walking and scrambling leads to the higher but less interesting summit of Dickey. Descend the backside across low-angle aprons of granite—carefully following the yellow blazes and cairns—and along the top of a cliff, with views across to Dickey and Welch. Then enter the woods for the final descent on a pleasant path.

3¼ hours, 4.5 miles, total climb: 1,830'

Approach: Six miles from Campton, turn left off NH 49 onto Upper Mad River Road. At Orris Road (0.7 mile) turn right, reaching the trailhead on the right at 1.3 miles.

Greeley Ponds

A designated national scenic area, these attractive ponds are quite popular. The ponds are situated in the narrow notch between Mount Kancamagus and the East Peak of Osceola. From the Waterville Valley side, it is a 3-mile hike over easy terrain to the lower pond. Start on **Livermore Road**, but turn left onto the **Greeley Ponds Trail** at Depot Clearing, 0.3 mile from the parking lot. Proceed on a fine, almost level woods road which eventually turns into an equally fine trail; the stream crossings have bridges, making this excellent for skiers and bikers as well as hikers. Soon after entering the **Greeley Ponds Scenic Area** (at 2.6 miles), the trail to the lower pond leaves the graded path (left), crosses a stream, and comes out to the shores of the lower pond. The upper pond is a half mile farther. Beyond the upper pond, at the height of land, Mt. Osceola Trail (to East Peak) branches left. Continuing straight ahead from this intersection, Greeley Ponds Trail descends gentle grades for 1.2 miles to the Kancamagus Highway. See Chapter 12 for this approach to the ponds.

   3½ hours, 7 miles, 500' elevation gain (upper pond)
   Approach: *Start from the Livermore Road parking area.*

On Greeley Ponds Trail, 0.9 mile from Depot Clearing, a spur trail (0.8 mile) branches left to **Goodrich Rock**, one of New Hampshire's larger glacial erratics. The trip to Goodrich Rock from Waterville Valley is four miles round trip.

Maps: WVAIA; WODC; AMC: *#3 Crawford Notch-Sandwich Range; Map Adventures*; USGS: *Waterville Valley, Mt. Osceola, Mt. Tripyramid.*

Camping: *The Forest Service maintains three campgrounds in the Campton-Waterville Valley area. Campton Campground (58 sites) is on NH 49, two miles from Campton. Waterville Valley Campground (27 sites) is on Tripoli Road, at the entrance to Waterville Valley. The third campground, Osceola Vista, is two miles up Tripoli Road, near the base of Livermore Road. There are private campgrounds in Plymouth, Holderness, and Rumney.*

15 | Squam Lake and Lake Winnipesaukee

The area around Lake Winnipesaukee and smaller Squam Lake is known as the Lakes Region. Although it is primarily the boating, fishing and swimming that draw the many visitors during the summer months, there is some fine hiking here as well. The mountains are lower, but the rocky, open summits with great views of the nearby lakes and distant mountains conspire to make it worthwhile. The main concentration of trails is on the Squam Mountains, the small range just north of Squam Lake. The popular hikes on Belknap Mountain and Mount Major are at the southern end of Lake Winnipesaukee. We also describe Bald Knob, a prominent rock buttress on the western edge of the Ossipee Range.

Mt. Morgan (2,220') and Mt. Percival (2,212')

One of the more interesting hikes in the area, this loop along the Squam Range offers several excellent viewpoints of surrounding lakes and mountains. From the parking area (base of Mt. Morgan Trail) walk northeast 0.3 mile along NH 113 to the **Mt. Percival Trail**. Follow this over a mixture of easy and moderate terrain, passing a good viewpoint at 1.6 miles, before reaching the **Crawford-Ridgepole Trail** and Mount Percival's summit at 1.9 miles. At 0.1 mile from the summit, there is a spur trail (left) to a cave. From the summit head left (southwest) along the ridge for 0.8 mile to the junction with the Mount Morgan Trail. Take this to a cliff view or stay on the Crawford-Ridgepole Trail 0.1 mile to the summit of Mount Morgan. Continue along the ridge for 0.4 mile, where the **Mount Morgan Trail** branches left and descends to your starting point on NH 113, for a total hike of about five miles.

Loop variation: 3¼ hours, 5.1 miles, total climb: 1,400'

Approach: From I-93 exit 24, take US 3 and NH 25 to NH 113 (Holderness). The trailhead is 5.5 miles north on NH 113.

Note: A shorter version of the above hike is very popular—climb only Morgan, using the Mount Morgan Trail up and down.

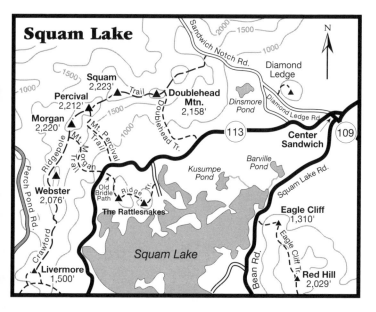

The Rattlesnakes 1,289'

Just across the road from the Mount Morgan trailhead is the area's most popular hike: the easy climb up **West Rattlesnake** (1,260'). From the parking area on NH 113 take **Old Bridle Path** (an old carriage road) for 0.8 mile to the rocks on top of West Rattlesnake. Squam Lake, with its many inlets and islands, spreads out 500 feet below. The smooth south-facing ledges are great for relaxing and contemplating life's mysteries. For many this may be exertion enough, but the easy 1-mile trip over to slightly higher **East Rattlesnake** will appeal to those looking for more of a hike. (Better views from West Rattlesnake.) Descend the way you came.

1 hour, 1.6 miles, total climb: 450'

Approach: As for the Mount Morgan Trail above, but the trail is on the south side of NH 113.

Note: There are a number of trails on the Rattlesnakes, and the Squam Lakes Association publishes an excellent map and guide.

Doublehead Mountain 2,158'

Doublehead Mountain is part of the Squam Mountains. It is a few miles east of Mt. Percival, to which it is connected by the **Crawford-Ridgepole Trail** (2 miles). To climb Doublehead directly from NH 113 walk out the old **Holderness-Sandwich Road** for about a mile, where the **Doublehead Trail** branches off to the right. After about 1.3 miles of moderate climbing, the reward of this hike is earned: an outstanding view of mountains and lakes—perhaps the best mountaintop view in the area. The summit of Doublehead is a short distance farther on, but the best view is from the lookout before the summit. Descend by the same route.

3 hours, 4.8 miles, total climb 1,320'
Approach: Park at the trailhead on NH 113, 3.5 miles west of Center Sandwich.

Eagle Cliff and Red Hill 2,029'

About 700' above the road, popular Eagle Cliff offers a stunning vistas of Squam Lake and surrounding coves and mountains. Follow the **Eagle Cliff Trail**; it climbs generally moderately (at times steeply) reaching two good lookouts at 0.6 miles. Return by the same route. For those who want a longer hike, continue to the top of Red Hill (2.5 miles). The firetower is staffed from April to October.

1 hour, 1.2 miles, total climb: 700' (Eagle Cliff only)
Approach: From Center Sandwich, drive south on Squam Lake Road 2.9 miles to the signed, but somewhat obscure trailhead.

Bald Knob and the Ossipee Range

Bald Knob (1,850') is the intriguing rock promontory high above the hamlet of Melvin Village, on the west side of the Ossipee Range. The Ossipee Range's compact and strangely circular shape—look at it on a good topo map—is due to its volcanic origin. The one-mile trail leaves Route 171 at the Moultonborough-Tuftonboro town line. At the unmarked trailhead, the posted sign apparently applies to hunters and not to hikers. Wend through an

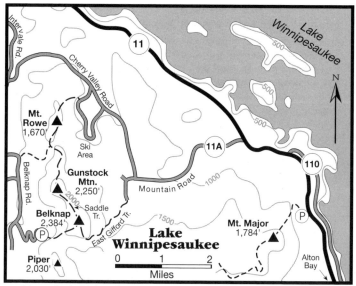

old sand pit before beginning a steady, rocky climb. Occasional white spray paint markings confirm your suspicions that you are on a trail. (The trail receives plenty of use and is easy to follow.) After ascending some fun slabs, you soon bear left and clamber up a short, steep section to the pleasant, grassy top with a carriage road turnaround. There are great views of Lake Winnipesaukee, especially late in the day. Descend the same way.

2 hours, 2 miles, total climb: 1,200'

Approach: *From Center Sandwich, drive south on NH 109 through Moultonborough and bear left on NH 171. Continue past Castle in the Clouds about a half-mile to the well-signed town line.*

Belknap Mountain 2,384'

This is a short, popular hike to an observation tower with great panoramic views. Although the various communication antennas detract from the experience, the view in all directions of the lake and mountains makes this trip worthwhile. From the picnic area,

take either the **Green Trail** or the **Red Trail**. The latter is the preferred route—it has a more comfortable grade, with better footing. The Green Trail has a power line running next to it. Descend
by either trail, although the Red Trail is easier.

1 hour, 1.4 miles, total climb: 690'

Approach: *From Gilford Village (east of Laconia) take Belknap
Mountain Road 2.4 miles to Belknap Carriage Road. Turn left and continue 1.5 miles to the trailhead.*

Gunstock Mountain 2,250'

In the summer, Gunstock Ski Area converts to a full-service campground and recreation area, offering mountain biking, horseback
riding, swimming and hiking. The **Brook Trail** and the **Flintlock
Trail** ascend Gunstock Mountain, using a combination of foot
trails, ski trails and ski service roads. Both start from the large
stone fireplace near the base of the Summit Triple Chairlift.
Ascending Brook Trail and descending on the Flintlock Trail
makes a good loop. For extra credit, follow the 1.3-mile **Saddle
Trail** from Gunstock's summit over to **Belknap Mountain**, where
the summit tower provides excellent views of Lake
Winnipesaukee and the surrounding area. Return by the same
route. A free sketch map showing Gunstock's system of hiking
and mountain bike trails is available at the campground.

2½ hours, 3.2 miles, total climb: 1,270' (Gunstock only)

Approach: *From exit 20 off I-93, continue to Laconia. Turn east onto NH
11A and continue a few miles to the Gunstock Recreation Area.*

Mount Major 1,784'

This is a popular, exciting hike to an open summit with sweeping
views of Lake Winnipesaukee, central New Hampshire, and into
Maine. Although it is a short hike and popular with families, the
mountain is quite steep with a couple of spots some hikers may
find a little difficult. At the outset the trail coincides with a jeep
road, branches off it and returns to it. After a brief level section,
the trail departs left from the jeep road and climbs steadily to the
summit. Rock slabs are ascended and views of the lake begin to

Overlooking Lake Winnipesaukee from Mount Major
Robert Kozlow

open up. There are a few, very short sections that require extra caution, especially on the descent and with small children. The wide-open summit area is spectacular and the old stone enclosure will provide relief from the cooling breeze. Take the same route back down.

2½ hours, 3 miles, total climb: 1,180'

Approach: The trailhead parking is on NH 11, 4.2 miles north of the village of Alton Bay, at the southeastern end of Lake Winnipesaukee.

Maps: USGS: *Center Sandwich, Laconia, Melvin Village, Squam Mountains, West Alton;* Squam Lake Association; Gunstock Ski Area.

Campgrounds: *Ellacoya State Park, White Lake State Park in West Ossipee. and Gunstock Recreation Area. Private campgrounds in Moultonborough, Holderness, and Weirs Beach (Laconia).*

16 Moosilauke-Hanover Area

The high, broad dome that is Mount Moosilauke is a prominent landmark, easily identified from many miles away. Although lacking the company of other high peaks, it receives plenty of attention from hikers. There are six routes up the mountain, none of them particularly easy. Even the shortest route takes about two hours. A procession of large cairns marks the Appalachian Trail as it traverses the large, grassy summit area. Because Moosilauke stands alone, the views in every direction are superb. The Dartmouth Outing Club maintains Moosilauke's trails and other trails in the region. Black Mountain, Mount Cube, and Smarts Mountain are also included in this chapter.

Mount Moosilauke (4,802') from Kinsman Notch

An interesting, longer route with much less traffic than the trails from Dartmouth's Ravine Lodge, the **Beaver Brook Trail** (AT south) climbs steadily and at times quite steeply along a plunging brook. Well-placed rungs and steps (wood blocks bolted to the rock) make for adequate foot and hand holds on the smooth slabs. After about 1½ hours you come to the 200' side trail (right) to **Beaver Brook Shelter**, where there is a view of Mt. Washington. After cresting the main ridge, the trail contours across Mt. Blue. Keep an eye out for raven acrobatics in wild **Jobildunk Ravine**, which drops away to the left. The final 10 minutes are across Moosilauke's open summit dome; follow the large cairns. Return by the same route.

6 hours, 6.8 miles, total climb: 2,910'

Approach: Drive to the height of land in Kinsman Notch, 13.5 miles east on NH 112 from NH 10 in Haverhill.

Mount Moosilauke from Ravine Lodge

Dartmouth College's Ravine Lodge lies at the foot of Moosilauke, and the traditional and most popular routes start from here. The lodge itself is primarily for the use of Dartmouth students and staff; it's also the field base of the Dartmouth Outing Club (DOC).

Leaning cairn on the summit of Mount Moosilauke   Robert Bailey

Gorge Brook and Snapper Trails

Although hiking up and down Gorge Brook is the common route on the mountain, the loop described here offers more variety and is a standard route as well. From the trailhead parking near **Ravine Lodge** (2,480'), drop down and cross the river. Following signs, stay on **Gorge Brook Trail** until you reach the **Snapper Trail**, 0.4 mile from the road. Originally cut as a ski trail, the Snapper Trail climbs moderately at first, then steeply, reaching the **Carriage Road** after a mile. Head right here and, after climbing steadily for another mile, you gain the summit ridge. **Glencliff Trail** comes in from the left, and the short side trip (left) to the open summit of South Peak is worthwhile. Continue over easy terrain to Moosilauke's expansive dome of a summit. On the descent, carefully follow signs for Gorge Brook Trail. Passing various outlooks, the trail descends briskly through woods to the Baker River crossing.

5 hours, 7.2 miles, total climb: 2,440'

Approach: From the intersection of NH 118 and NH 25 in Warren, drive northeast about 6 miles on NH 118 to Ravine Lodge Road. Hiker parking is just past the lodge, at the end of the road, about 1.6 miles from NH 118.

Mount Moosilauke via Benton Trail

The Benton Trail is a pleasant, although little-used route up this big mountain. From **Tunnel Brook Road**, the Benton Trail crosses a stream and ascends moderately, passing viewpoints at about 1.2 miles and 2.5 miles. The upper portion of the trail climbs through spruce and fir, breaking into the open a few minutes before the actual summit. Return by the same route. This is considered the easiest way to climb Moosilauke, but with an elevation gain of over 3,000', it will give most hikers a very thorough workout.

5–6 hours, 6.8 miles, total climb: 3,110'

Approach: From NH 112 (just east of the NH 112/NH 116 intersection) take Tunnel Brook Road south. At 1.4 miles bear left and continue 1.5 miles to the trailhead.

Glencliff Trail and the Carriage Road

The three-mile long Glencliff Trail ties into the Carriage Road, which then traverses the final mile of this route across the high ridge between South Peak and the actual summit. From the car, walk through a pasture before picking up an old logging road and commencing the climb up **South Peak**. The last half mile before the Carriage Road is steep. A five-minute spur trail (right) leads to the top of South Peak, where there are good views. With little climbing remaining, head left on the Carriage Road to the top. See the skiing chapter for more information on the Carriage Road.

6 hours, 8.2 miles, total climb: 3,300'

Approach: From Glencliff on NH 25 take the road to the N.H. Home for the Elderly (1.2 miles) and the hiker parking area.

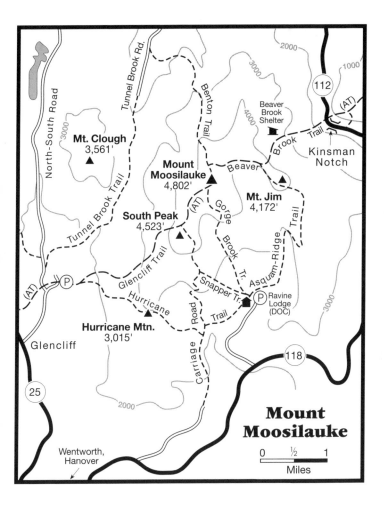

North-South Road

Tunnel Brook Rd.

2000
1000
112
(AT)

3000

Mt. Clough
3,561'

Benton Trail

Beaver
Brook
Shelter

Beaver

4000

Brook

Trail

Kinsman
Notch

Mount
Moosilauke
4,802'

Tunnel Brook Trail

(AT)

Gorge

Mt. Jim
4,172'

South Peak
4,523'

Brook

Asquam-Ridge

Tr.

Trail

(AT)
P

Glencliff Trail

Snapper Tr.

P   Ravine
Lodge
(DOC)

Hurricane

3000

Carriage

Trail

Hurricane Mtn.
3,015'

Road

Glencliff

118

25

2000

**Mount
Moosilauke**

0   ½   1

Miles

Wentworth,
Hanover

Hikes in the Hanover area

The four hikes described below are local favorites for folks in the Hanover-Upper Valley area. Black Mountain, in particular, is a rewarding hike for little effort. Mount Ascutney in Vermont is a steep mountain with wide views from its observation platform.

Black Mountain 2,836'

Black Mountain's rocky summit is quite prominent from NH 25 when approached from the west. After passing through a low boggy area, the well-used **Haverhill Heritage Trail** (Chippewa Trail) touches briefly on a woods road before getting down to business. About 20 minutes out it begins a steep climb through a spruce forest. Pay attention to the yellow blazes, as the trail is occasionally vague. The final third of the hike is on bare rock slabs or ledge, with good intermittent views. Scramble across the rocky ridgecomb to the summit with its unobstructed views south and west

3 hours, 4.5 miles, total climb: 1,000'

Approach: From Haverhill drive east on NH 25 to East Haverhill, turn left on Lime Kiln Road, and continue 3 miles—stay left at a "Y" intersection—to a parking spot on the right.

Mount Cube 2,909'

This popular mountain has great views from its rocky north summit. It is a traditional first hike for many families. From NH 25A, follow the **Appalachian Trail** south as it leads through a wet area, crosses a small road, and after climbing about 800 feet, drops down and crosses a brook. From here the trail switchbacks about 1000 feet up the east flank of Mount Cube, reaching a trail junction 3.1 miles from the road. Head right at this T-junction for 0.2 mile (climbing 200') to get to the north and higher summit where, on a good day, fine views of nearby Moosilauke await. Return by the same route.

4½ hours, 6.6 miles, total climb: 2,200'

Approach: From Orford, drive east on NH 25A for 10 miles to the Appalachian Trail crossing. Park east of the bridge.

Smarts Mountain 3,240'

Popular **Lambert Ridge Trail** ascends Smarts Mountain from the south, providing a solid hike with good viewpoints and a tower at the summit. It is also a segment of the AT. From the road ascend moderately through hardwoods on a good trail, reaching a viewpoint after a half hour. After another mile (at 1.8 miles), there's an enticing view of the summit. Descend briefly before tackling the steeper upper mountain. At the summit area the DOC's tent platforms and shelter are popular camping spots, and the views from the old fire tower are excellent. Mount Cube is seven miles to the north via the Appalachian Trail.

> *5 hours, 7.4 miles, total climb: 2,400'*
> *Approach: From Lyme drive east to the Dartmouth Skiway. Bear left on Dorchester Rd. and continue 1.6 miles to a small parking area on the left.*

Mount Ascutney (Vermont) 3,150'

Just across the Connecticut River from Claremont, steep-sided Mount Ascutney offers some of the best hiking in the region. The interesting, varied **Brownsville Trail** provides a very worthwhile hike to Ascutney's fine observation platform. After starting out very steeply, the grade slackens and the trail passes through an abandoned granite quarry. An awkward, rocky section is followed by a pleasant, steady climb. Eventually the Brownsville Trail merges with **Windsor Trail** and, at an old foundation 0.2 miles from the top, a spur trail leads right to a clifftop and a birds-eye view of the country north of Ascutney. From the summit platform most of Vermont's major mountains are visible, as well as a wide swath of New Hampshire. Return by the same route.

> *4½ hours, 6.4 miles, total climb: 2,400'*
> *Approach: From Windsor, Vermont (on I-91, south of White River Jct.), drive 4.6 miles west on Rt. 44 to a parking area on the left.*

Maps: AMC #4 *Moosilauke-Kinsman*; Wilderness: *Kancamagus Highway;* Map Adventures: *VT-NH Hiking*; USGS: *East Haverhill, Mount Ascutney, Mount Moosilauke, Piermont, Smarts Mountain.*

Campgrounds: *There are private campgrounds in Rumney, Wentworth, Warren, Orford, and Woodstock.*

Hypothermia

Hypothermia is a fairly serious threat to hikers and can prove fatal, so it is important to understand it, and how to avoid it. Hypothermia occurs when a person's core body temperature drops below normal, i.e the body is no longer able to maintain its warmth. Symptoms include disorientation, slurring of speech, hallucinations, and sleepiness. The best way to avoid hypothermia and its serious consequences is by using common sense. Plan your trip carefully—assess the condtion and ablilities of all members of your group realistically. Anticipate worse weather/delays by bringing extra food and clothing. Layer your clothing, so that you can better regulate your comfort level by adding or taking off a layer: you want to avoid being drenched in sweat as you crest a ridge, only to meet an icy wind. Polypropylene and wool will keep you warm when wet, whereas cotton will not. Wearing a warm hat is essential, since we lose a significant amount of heat from our heads. Resting against rocks or sitting on the ground drains body heat.

On long, tiring trips be on the watch for the early warning signs of hypothermia—shivering, extreme fatigue, poor coordination, illogicalness—and consider turning back or taking immediate action. Overexertion combined with cold and/or wet conditions set the stage for hypothermia. Warm drinks will help raise the body temperature, but it is imperative to get a hypothermia victim indoors or to a warm environment as soon as possible.

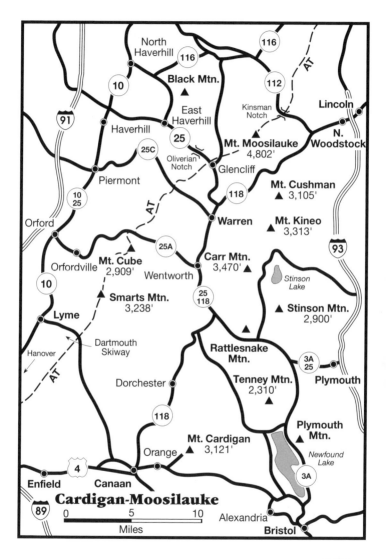

North Haverhill

116

10

Black Mtn. ▲

East Haverhill

25

25C

Piermont

10 25

91

Orford

Orfordville

10

Lyme

AT

Hanover

AT

Mt. Cube 2,909' ▲

Smarts Mtn. 3,238' ▲

Dartmouth Skiway

Dorchester ●

118

Orange

Mt. Cardigan 3,121' ▲

Enfield ●

89

4

Canaan

116

112

Kinsman Notch

Lincoln

N. Woodstock

Mt. Moosilauke 4,802'

Oliverian Notch

Glencliff

Mt. Cushman 3,105' ▲

118

Warren ●

25A

Mt. Kineo 3,313' ▲

93

Carr Mtn. 3,470' ▲

Wentworth

25 118

Stinson Lake

Stinson Mtn. 2,900' ▲

▲

Rattlesnake Mtn. ▲

Tenney Mtn. 2,310' ▲

3A 25

Plymouth ●

Plymouth Mtn. ▲

Newfound Lake

3A

Cardigan-Moosilauke

0   5   10
Miles

Alexandria

Bristol ●

17 Mount Cardigan–Rumney Area

Although not the highest mountain in the area, nor the only one with an open summit, Cardigan is easily the most popular. At a little over 3,000' it is not above treeline, but a fire in the 1800s has left us with a beautiful rock dome of a summit. Partly because of this, it is a favorite beginner's hike. Many a New England hiker started out here! The mountain has an extensive network of trails. On the east side, the AMC's Cardigan Lodge is the starting point for a variety of hiking routes and cross country ski trails. The chapter concludes with two hikes near Lake Stinson and one on Rattlesnake Mountain, just west of Rumney village. The map on the previous page shows the location of these mountains.

Mount Cardigan (3,121') from the west

From the picnic area, follow the **West Ridge Trail**. This popular trail ascends at an easy angle, meeting several other trails along the way. The upper portion is across bare ledges which soon lead to the wide open summit, with its panoramic vista. The small fire-tower is manned. Descend by the same route. A variation is to take the **Clark Trail** south from the summit, soon meeting **South Ridge Trail**. Then head right and descend to the parking area.

2 hours, 3 miles, total climb: 1,220'

Approach: From Canaan (near I-89 and Enfield) drive north 0.5 mile on NH 118. Turn right, follow signs, and continue through Orange to Cardigan State Park and the trailhead.

Mount Cardigan from Cardigan Lodge

From Cardigan Lodge on the east side of the mountain, the standard ascent is a 2.6-mile combination of the **Holt**, **Cathedral Forest**, and **Clark Trails**. From the lodge, follow the Holt Trail for 1.1 miles to a trail intersection called **Grand Junction**. Head left onto Cathedral Forest Trail and follow it for 0.6 mile, where it merges with the Clark Trail. Bear right and continue on Clark for 0.9 mile to the summit. The climb will take a little over 2 hours. Make your descent either by the same route or, for an interesting and slightly longer variation, take the **Mowglis Trail** over to **Firescrew**, the north summit. It is 0.6 mile across; the trail dips down a bit, emerging on the open top of Firescrew with a great view back to Cardigan. Now leave the Mowglis Trail (keep right) and pick up **Manning Trail**, following it back down to the Holt Trail. Then head left over easy ground to Cardigan Lodge.

> ***For the loop trip: 4 hours, 5.6 miles, total climb: 1,850'***
> ***Approach:*** *Two miles north of Bristol, turn left off Route 3A at Newfound Lake. Two miles from the lake, proceed straight through the intersection. Then head right at three miles and left at 6.3 miles. Keep right, reaching the lodge nine miles from the lake.*

Final pitch on the Holt Trail, Mount Cardigan   Jared Gange

The Holt Trail on Cardigan

The upper portion of the Holt Trail, one of the most challenging routes in the White Mountains, is an exhilarating climb—especially on a warm summer day. The trail starts from Cardigan lodge. At the trail intersection called **Grand Junction** (1.1 miles) continue straight ahead on the Holt Trail, paralleling the brook. The trail steepens, soon ascending a seemingly vertical but not especially difficult gully. Work your way up enjoyable slabs and ledges. Just below the summit the slabs are steep and exposed. Do not attempt this route when it is wet or icy! Descend by the Clark–Cathedral Forest–Holt combination or by the Mowglis and Manning Trails (over Firescrew) as described above.

3½ hours, 4.8 miles, total climb: 1,750'

Approach: Cardigan Lodge is nine miles east of Newfound Lake, off Route 3A. See directions on the previous page.

Cardigan Lodge

The AMC's Cardigan Lodge offers meals and dormitory lodging during the summer and fall seasons. Tent platforms are also available. From late fall to late spring the lodge may be rented by groups on a self-service basis. In addition to the fine hiking on Mount Cardigan, there is a long tradition of skiing at Cardigan Lodge, where the AMC holds ski clinics. Contact the AMC for more information. See the skiing chapter for information on the Alexandria and Duke Ski Trails.

Plymouth Mountain 2,187'

Located between Bristol and Plymouth, Plymouth Mountain offers a moderate hike. A viewpoint just below the summit gives good views of Newfound Lake and nearby Mount Cardigan. From the top, continue a short distance to a clearing facing toward the northeast and Franconia Ridge. Descend the same trail.

2½ hours, 3 miles, total climb: 900'

Approach: When driving north on Route 3A from Bristol, turn right (east) on Pike Hill Road at the north end of Newfound Lake. Proceed 1.4 miles to the trailhead on the right.

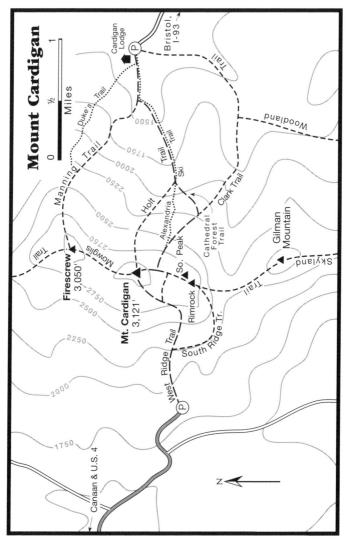

Mount Cardigan

Miles
0   ½   1

Cardigan Lodge P

Bristol, I-93

Trail

Woodland

Duke's Trail

1500

Trail Trail

1750

Ski

2000

Manning Trail

2250

Holt

Clark Trail

2500

Alexandria

Cathedral Forest Trail

Gilman Mountain

2750

Mowgli's

So. Peak

Skyland Trail

Trail

Firescrew 3,050'

2750

Mt. Cardigan 3,121'

Rimrock

2500

West Ridge Trail

South Ridge Tr.

2250

2000

N

1750

Canaan & U.S. 4

Stinson Mountain 2,900'

The top of Stinson Mountain offers good views from its partially open summit. From the parking area, the **Stinson Mountain Trail** starts out on easy terrain. It soon steepens, switchbacking up the mountainside to the rocky summit. Once on the top, find the side path that leads to an opening for more views. Descend by the same route.

2½ hours, 3.5 miles, total climb: 1,400'

Approach: *From Rumney (on NH 25), drive five miles up Stinson Lake Road to Stinson Lake. Head right for 0.8 mile on Cross Road. Turn right and park on the left after 0.3 mile.*

Carr Mountain 3,470'

The hike up Carr Mountain is somewhat longer than Stinson Mountain. There are good views from the rocks at the summit area.From the trailhead parking, follow **Three Ponds Trail** for 0.5 mile to the **Carr Mountain Trail**. Turn left here and cross Sucker Brook. This may prove difficult during periods of heavy runoff. The trail climbs generally moderately; take the side trail to the left to reach the summit. Descend by the same route.

4 hours, 6.4 miles, total climb: 1,940'

Approach: *From the southern end of Stinson Lake, five miles north of Rumney, continue on the main road along the lake for two miles to the hiker parking area on the left.*

Rattlesnake Mountain 1,594'

Quite prominent from the highway, the open ledges of Rattlesnake Mountain provide great views of the Baker River Valley. From Buffalo Road, **Rattlesnake Mountain Trail** climbs, at times steeply, reaching the loop trail over the summit after a mile and the open ledges at 1.4 miles. The total distance for the loop hike is 2.5 miles. Descend by the same trail.

2 hours, 2.5 miles, total climb: 840'

Approach: *In Rumney village (just off NH 25) head left on Buffalo Road for 2.5 miles to roadside parking. The trailhead is on the right.*

Drinking Water

"Water, water everywhere, and not a drop fit to drink without treating it first" to paraphrase Coleridge. This is putting things in a murky light, but unfortunately the now widespread Giardia parasite leads to the conclusion that no surface water—lake or stream—can be assumed safe to drink, untreated. Giardia is found throughout the U.S. and the rest of the world. Animals carry the parasite in their intestines, and pass it through feces. In human digestive tracts, the parasite causes a variety of unpleasant symptoms: stomach cramps, gas, and diarrhea, to name a few. The symptoms may pass after several days, but in some cases, a chronic condition develops. You want to avoid this! Boiling water for five minutes is an effective treatment, as are iodine purification tablets. Most of the good water filters do an adequate job of removing the parasite. For day hikes, most hikers carry with them whatever they plan to drink during their hike. Campers can do their part by doing all of their washing at least 200 feet from streams and ponds.

Note: See the area map on page 167 for the general locations of Plymouth, Stinson, Carr and Rattlesnake Mountains.

Maps: AMC: *Cardigan, #4 Moosilauke-Kinsman*; USGS: *Ashland, Mt. Cardigan, Mt. Kineo, Newfound Lake, Rumney.*

Camping: Private campgrounds in Rumney, Bristol, Plymouth, and Warren.

18 Mt. Monadnock and So. New Hampshire

For the southern part of New Hampshire—generally the area below I-89 in the western portion and south of Lake Winnipesaukee in the eastern portion—we present 14 of the most popular hikes, including six routes up Mount Monadnock. The summits here are lower than in the north but the trips described lead to mountain tops with excellent views. The better-known mountains in this group are Monadnock, Kearsarge, Sunapee, Pack Monadnock, and the Uncanoonucs. New Hampshire's southern landmark, Mount Monadnock, with its great rock summit, is immensely popular; it is one of the most climbed mountains in the world. These mountains provide good beginner hiking. And because the peaks are lower and farther south, the season is longer than for the mountains to the north.

Mount Sunapee 2,743'

Great views of lakes and the surrounding mountains are the draw of this hike. The **Andrew Brook Trail** starts out very gently and then climbs moderately through woods to reach the north end of peaceful **Lake Solitude**. Head right for a few minutes to the orange-blazed **Monadnock–Sunapee Greenway**. Turn right, and make the short climb to **White Ledge** (2,700') with its clifftop view of Lake Solitude and nearby lakes and mountains. From here it is an easy 1.3 miles on to the summit, complete with snackbar and chairlift. Since the view from White Ledge is so good, many hikers let this be their end destination.

> *5 hours, 6.8 miles, total climb: 1,550' (to the summit)*
> *Approach: On NH 103, one mile south of Newbury (south end of Lake Sunapee), take Mountain Road 1.2 miles to the trailhead on the right.*

Note: A popular and much easier way to climb Mount Sunapee is to ride up the ski area's chairlift and walk down the ski runs. Mt. Sunapee's **Summit Trail** begins at the base of the ski area and runs two miles to the top.

Lake Solitude from White Ledge, Mount Sunapee   Jared Gange

Mount Kearsarge 2,937'

The various communication antennas cannot spoil this summit with its fine views in all directions. In clear weather Sunapee, Cardigan, Moosilauke, Franconia Ridge, Mount Washington, and many other mountains are visible. Mount Kearsarge has two trails: the half-mile route from the south (from Rollins State Park) and the longer **Wilmot Trail** (Northside Trail) from Winslow State Park, described here. From the upper end of the picnic area, pick up the trail—it's well-worn, and hard to miss. A little over halfway, after a short, very steep section, the grade eases, the trail leads across smooth rock slabs, and the view gradually opens up. Total distance to the summit is only 1.1 miles. Descend by the same route.

> *1¾ hours, 2.2 miles, total climb: 1,100'*
>
> ***Approach:*** *From I-89 exit 10, follow the signs to Winslow State Park (six miles). Turn left on Kearsarge Valley Road, then right on Kearsarge Mountain Road, and follow it to the state park.*

Lovewell Mountain 2,469'

Walk up the old 4WD road, noting the white blazes of the **Monadnock–Sunapee Greenway**. Continue in an easterly direction for a mile, where the trail heads left and commences its steeper ascent. Climb up across pleasant mixed terrain, the trail at times marked by cairns, reaching the summit 2.5 miles from the car. Descent is by the same route.

2¾ hours, 4.5 miles, total climb: 930'

Approach: At 8.3 miles from Route 9 in Hillsboro on NH 31, turn right onto Mill Street, which turns into Halfmoon Pond Road. At 1.5 miles, park where a rough 4WD road heads right.

Oak Hill 970'

From the enclosed firetower on the top, a good number of southern New Hampshire's heights can be seen: Mount Monadnock, the Uncanoonucs, Sunapee, and Kearsarge, as well as the golden capitol dome about 5 miles away in Concord. Follow the firetower access road, reaching the top after a mile. This is a pleasant woods walk, popular with families. Stay on the jeep road the entire way.

1¼ hours, 2 miles, total climb: 400'

Approach: From I-93 exit 16, just north of Concord, head east on Shamut (Oak Hill) Road four miles to a gated road on the left.

Blue Job Mountain 1,356'

A popular family hike, Blue Job Mountain affords great views from an isolated, open summit. On a clear day the views from the lookout tower stretch all the way from Mount Washington to Boston and out to the Atlantic. The half-mile trail (unmarked, but easy to follow) to the top offers fun woods walking mixed with passages across granite ledges and scrambles around boulders.

45 minutes to 1 hour, 1 mile, total climb: 400'

Approach: From Rochester, take NH 202A west (4.2 miles) to First Crown Point Road; bear right and continue for 5.4 miles to parking on the right.

Pawtuckaway State Park

As one of the larger natural areas (5,500 acres) in southern New Hampshire, Pawtuckaway State Park offers some pleasant short hikes. The network of park roads is not well marked, so it is a good idea to obtain a copy of the free park map to figure out road access and trail locations.

The **Boulder Field**, an impressive collection of huge glacial erratics, is popular with rock climbers and hikers alike. It is accessed by the 0.8-mile **Boulder Trail** (sign) off Round Pond Road, which is to the left off Reservation Road.

Probably the most popular hike is **South Mountain** (908'). The 60-foot lookout tower on its summit enhances the view considerably, bringing most of southern New Hampshire under scrutiny. Take Reservation Road to Tower Road and turn left. From here several trails ascend South Mountain.

Approach: From Deerfield (east of Concord), head south for 2.7 miles on NH 107 to get to Reservation Road. The park's main entrance is on Mountain Road, off NH 156.

North Uncanoonuc 1,324'

South Uncanoonuc has a road up it and the top is crammed with antennas and such. Nearby, higher North Uncanoonuc is much less developed and has a fine trail to its semi-open summit. Follow the **White Circle Trail**, marked with white circles, as it climbs quite steeply, with occasional good views through openings in the forest. Return by the same trail.

1½ hours, 1.5 miles, total climb: 730'
Approach: Take NH 114 west from Manchester to Goffstown and turn south on Mountain Road. The trailhead is on the right side of the road, 1.9 miles from NH 114.

Crotched Mountain 2,055'

For a hike that gives fine views for relatively little effort, this trip is ideal. The views are of Mount Sunapee, Mount Monadnock, and much of the southern part of the state. Starting out as a gravel road, the route stays left at the first two forks, climbing gently. As it climbs up through blueberry bushes, great views to the south open up. Upon gaining the ridge, head left on the trail; the summit, with its abandoned fire tower, is a short distance farther on. Although low, Crotched Mountain is the local high point, and has excellent views in all directions. Descend by the same route. Note that there are two other trails off the top.

2¾ hours, 4 miles, total climb: 750'

Approach: From Greenfield, drive north on NH 31 one mile, then bear right for 1.6 miles, passing the Crotched Mountain Rehabilitation Center. Park just ahead along the road on the left at a gate.

Pack Monadnock 2,288'

Pack Monadnock has two main summits, North Pack and South Pack. The hike given here is along the ridge joining the two summits. Drive up South Pack and, from the picnic area, head north on the **Wapack Trail**, marked by yellow triangles. The trail descends to a boggy section, then climbs up and over **Middle Peak** to limited views. The final switchbacking climb up **North Pack** (2,278') leads to good views from the large, relatively flat summit, especially of nearby **Mount Monadnock**. Return by the same route.

3 hours, 4.6 miles, total climb: 1,320'

Approach: From Peterborough, drive east on NH 101 four miles to Miller State Park, on the left.

The Wapack Trail

The yellow-blazed Wapack Trail runs for 22 miles from **Mount Watatic** in Ashburnham, Massachusetts, across Barrett and Temple Mountains and traverses the north-south ridge of Pack Monadnock before ending just north of **North Pack Monadnock** in Greenfield, New Hampshire. Starting from Massachusetts Route 119, it reaches Watatic's summit after 1.2 miles, crosses NH 123 at 9 miles, and crosses NH 101 near Peterborough, at the base of Pack Monadnock, after 16 miles.

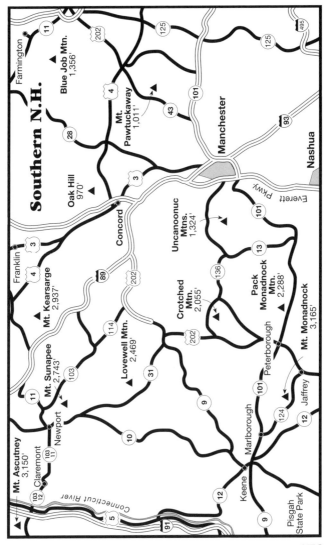

Southern N.H.

Farmington
Blue Job Mtn. 1,356'
Mt. Pawtuckaway 1,011'
Manchester
Nashua
Oak Hill 970'
Concord
Franklin
Uncanoonuc Mtns. 1,324'
Everett Pkwy.
Mt. Kearsarge 2,937'
Crotched Mtn. 2,055'
Pack Monadnock Mtn. 2,288'
Mt. Sunapee 2,743'
Lovewell Mtn. 2,469'
Peterborough
Mt. Monadnock 3,165'
Mt. Ascutney 3,150'
Newport
Claremont
Jaffrey
Marlborough
Connecticut River
Keene
Pisgah State Park

Mount Monadnock 3,165'

The most climbed mountain in the United States? Probably. With excellent trails approaching its rocky, open summit from every direction, Monadnock seems able to withstand the onslaught of the hikers it attracts; about 125,000 a year. Its fantastic summit—itself a miniature mountain of steep, bare rock—is one of the finest in New Hampshire. Located in Jaffrey (near Keene), in the far southern part of the state, and only about 90 minutes from Boston, Monadnock represents the closest, highest mountain for a large number of hikers. It is not a trivial mountain, and even athletic hikers will find themselves rushed to make the top in under an hour. The most popular starting point is Monadnock State Park.

Main Route: The White Dot Trail

White Dot Trail is the most direct route, and it is by far the most heavily used. From the parking area, follow the wide, rocky path across easy terrain, reaching the branch left to White Cross Trail after 0.5 mile, and at 0.7 mile, **Falcon Spring**, where Cascade Link branches right. From here upwards, the trail is steeper—at times handholds as well as footholds are needed—and it runs almost continuously over bare rock. Note that in places, the rock has been worn smooth and slippery by the passage of hundreds of thousands of hikers. The upper third of the route is almost completely out in the open, and the summit beckons. This is one of the finest stretches of hiking in New England! With good visibility, Boston's skyline stands out nicely. Descend the way you came up, following the white dots. The White Cross Trail provides a somewhat longer and more scenic variation on the White Dot Trail.

3 hours, 4.4 miles, elevation gain: 1,800'
Approach: About two miles west of Jaffrey, turn off NH 124 and follow the Monadnock State Park signs two miles to the hiker parking area.

Red Spot variation: For a longer and steeper variation on the above, bear right on **Cascade Link**, reaching the **Red Spot Trail** after a half mile. This very rocky, and at times quite steep trail eventually comes into the open a few minutes before meeting the **Pumpelly Trail**. Stay left on it to the top. Descend White Dot Trail.

White Dot Trail and Cascade Link

For a slightly longer variation on the usual route, consider the following, somewhat off the beaten path. Follow White Dot for 0.7 mile to Falcon Spring. Head north here on **Cascade Link** for about a mile to the **Pumpelly Trail**, where fine views open up. To the east, views are of woods, ledges, the ridge to North Pack Monadnock and, on a clear day, Boston. This is a good lunch spot. Now head west (left) along the Pumpelly Trail, with its 180-degree views, reaching the summit after another 1.4 miles. The easiest and most direct descent route is via the White Dot or White Cross trail. A more energetic option is to descend the way you came. Either way, pay close attention to trailmarkers.

3½ hours, 5.2 miles, climb: 1,800' (descending White Dot Trail)
Approach: *From Monadnock State Park.*

Trails in the Halfway House area

Describing the many side trails in the vicinity of the Halfway House Site is beyond the scope of this guide. The Cliff Walk, described next, crosses nine of these minor trails.

Cliff Walk

Considered by some to be the most beautiful of the trails on Monadnock, the Cliff Walk is a historic route as well. Both Thoreau and Emerson spent time meditating from its heights. Views extend south to Little Monadnock and the Quabbin Reservoir, and southwest to Mount Greylock. From the Halfway House parking, start up the Old Toll Road and, after about 0.6 mile, bear right on the **Parker Trail**. (It connects to the State Park campground). After 0.4 mile on the Parker Trail, branch left onto Cliff Walk. Carefully following the white "C's" painted on rocks, make the somewhat circuitous climb, reaching **Bald Rock**—good views—after about 1.5 miles. Continue through a trail intersection to reach the **White Arrow Trail** (marked with white arrows), and follow it to the top. Descend the via White Arrow Trail and the Old Toll Road.

3¾ hours, 5.6 miles, total climb: about 1,800'
Approach: *Park at the base of the Old Toll Road, five miles west of Jaffrey.*

Hard to get lost on this trail!   Jared Gange

White Arrow Trail

This trail ascends directly and steeply, crossing ledges before reaching the summit. To reach the White Arrow Trail, walk 1.2 miles up the Old Toll Road (closed to cars) to the Halfway House Site. From here, the White Arrow Trail (marked with white arrows) leads to the summit in only 1.1 miles. After an intersection about halfway the trail soon passes out of the trees onto the open ledges of the upper mountain. The Dublin and Marlboro trails join White Arrow just before the top. Descend by the same route.

> *3¼ hours, 4.6 miles, total climb: 1,665'*
>
> *Approach: From Jaffrey, drive west five miles on NH 124 to the parking lot at the base of the Old Toll Road.*

Marlboro Trail

This out-in-the-open trail ascends Mount Monadnock from the west. Starting out very moderately, in a forest strewn with huge

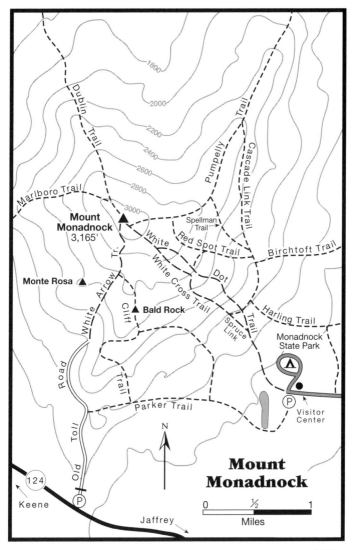

1800
2000
2200
2400
2600
2800
3000

Dublin Trail

Marlboro Trail

Mount Monadnock
3,165'

Monte Rosa ▲

White Arrow Tr.

Cliff

▲ Bald Rock

White Cross Trail

White

Red Spot Trail

Spellman Trail →

Pumpelly Trail

Cascade Link Trail

Birchtoft Trail

Dot

Harling Trail

Trail

Spruce Link

Monadnock State Park

Visitor Center

P

Road

Old Toll

Trail

Parker Trail

N

(124)

← Keene

Jaffrey →

P

Mount Monadnock

0   ½   1
Miles

boulders, the trail soon steepens and breaks out onto bare ledges. As is typical for the upper mountain, the route ascends in a step-like fashion, alternating between forest pockets and steeper ledge sections. About a half mile from the top the summit area comes into view, and about 10 minutes from the top, the Dublin Trail merges from the left, followed shortly by the White Arrow Trail from the right. After enjoying the view, descend by the same route, carefully noting the markings at the various trail forks.

3 hours, 4.4 miles, total climb: 1,865'

Approach: From Marlborough drive five miles east on NH 124 to Shaker Farm Road on the left. Park after 0.7 mile. The road is quite rough. Approaching from the east, Shaker Farm Road is 7.3 miles west of Jaffrey.

Pumpelly Trail

With its stunning 180-degree views—Mount Washington is visible on a clear day—the longest route on Monadnock is worth the extra time and effort. Plan for a full day of hiking. For the first 1.5 miles or so, the path is a mix of road and trail. About 0.3 mile further on, the trail bears to the left and steepens as it ascends a ridge. In about another mile the trail gets rougher as it leads across ledges. This area has superb views. At about 3 miles Cascade Link enters from the left. (It descends to the White Dot Trail and State Park Headquarters.) Now marked by cairns, the trail works its way onward and upward, bearing sharply right where the Spellman Trail comes up from the left from Cascade Link. (See map.) Continue over increasingly open and ledgy terrain to the summit. Note the various trail intersections as you ascend the mountain, so that on your return trip you make the right choices. The trail is generally well-marked, but you will need to pay attention. Because this is a long trip, be sure to take plenty of food and water. Descend the way you came, by the Pumpelly Trail.

5-6 hours, 8.8 miles, total climb: 1,700'

Approach: Drive west from Dublin on NH 101 0.4 mile, then head left on East Lake Road and park after 0.4 mile.

Camping: State Parks: Mt. Monadnock, Bear Brook, and Pawtuckaway. Private campgrounds in Keene, Fitzwilliam, Rindge, Goshen, and Hancock.

Hikers approach the summit of Mount Monadnock   Jared Gange

Mount Monadnock State Park

The park is open year round and park rangers are on hand every day. They will be able to answer your questions and to provide you with the Department of State Parks' excellent topographic map which shows the hiking trails. A day usage fee is charged for persons over 12 years old.

Maps: State Park Map; AMC; USGS: *Andover, Baxter Lake, Goffstown, Marlborough, Monadnock, Mt. Pawtuckaway, Lovewell Mtn., Newport, Penacook, Peterborough No., Peterborough So., Pinardville, Warner.*

19 Hiking in Winter

Sparkling snow crystals in brilliant sunshine, snow-laden boughs slapping you in the face, clear air with incredible mountain views, wallowing in deep snow, unable to locate a trail familiar in summer—these are the facts of winter hiking. There is a lot of hiker activity during the snowy months, and it is on the increase: most of the popular summer trails are travelled in winter. On most Saturdays in winter there are probably a half-dozen hikes organized by various AMC chapters.

With proper gear and a little instruction, winter hiking is safe and enjoyable. Some pointers:

Daylight: There is much less of it! Especially in early winter (December and January). Plan accordingly. Always take a flashlight or headlamp with fresh batteries. Know how much daylight you have to work with and allow some extra time.

Weather: There is more of it...more stormy weather, at any rate. Pay very close attention to weather forecasts, especially for trips above treeline.

Trail conditions vary enormously—far more than in summer. As you hike along, snow texture can change from powder to slush to ice in a matter of minutes, because of changes in elevation, temperature, and exposure to sun and shade.

Trail markers are much harder to follow in winter. Paint blazes can be covered by snow or be too low to easily notice. Bear in mind that most trails are not cut for winter travel—walking on top of four or five feet of snow, it is often very difficult to follow the trail. Hence the leader must know the route well.

Equipment: Be prepared with snowshoes or skis. Regardless the conditions at the trailhead early in the day, conditions higher up, or later in the day, are often quite different. The woods-protected trail leading up to a ridge may offer firm, packed snow, making for rapid progress. However, once on the exposed summit ridge, the trail can be covered with deep drifts, alternating with glare ice. Generally, snowshoes are much more appropriate than skis. Although this is not so much a factor when ascending, the

Winter hiker consulting with feathered friend   Richard Bailey

narrowness and steepness of most trails makes snowshoes the obvious choice for the descent.

Contingencies: Because there is a greater chance of something going wrong, and because a quick return to the trailhead is sometimes not possible—even over relatively short distances—it is a good idea to take bivouac equipment on trips more than 3-4 miles from the road.

Access: A number of the approach roads are gated in winter, adding to the total effort and seriousness of some trips. For example, any of the trips using Zealand Road for access are seven miles longer (round trip) in winter.

Ice can be a significant factor, especially in the fall and any time there is little or no snow cover. Crampons are essential at times. But even with crampons, an element of danger is often present, requiring experience on the part of the hiker. However *some* ice is unavoidable, and most of the time crampons are not needed: just a watchful eye and experience walking on the stuff. Crampons tend to be overused—kept on longer than needed—causing damage to tree roots and scarring rocks.

Recommended Winter Trips

For information on driving approaches and trail distances for the trips given below, see their respective chapters.

Carter Notch Hut About an eight-mile round trip on generally moderate terrain, via Nineteen Mile Brook Trail. A very popular snowshoe excursion, but somewhat difficult for skiers in the vicinity of the ridge. The hut is open all winter.

Hermit Lake Follow the heavily-used Tuckerman Ravine Trail for 2.4 miles to Hermit Lake with its dramatic views of the ravine. This one can usually be done without snowshoes.

Kearsarge North A good beginner winter trip. There are great views from the tower on the summit. Six miles round trip.

Zealand Falls Hut A very popular snowshoe or ski. It is one of the best introductory backcountry ski trips in the state. A very easy road section is followed by a pleasant, gentle climb to the hut. The last 10 minutes are steep—skiers remove their skis and walk this portion. See the ski chapter for more information.

Lonesome Lake Popular short hike in the Franconia Notch area. It is about 1.5 miles and 1–2 hours to the lake from Lafayette Place. Good views of Franconia Ridge across the valley.

More Difficult Winter Trips

Tripyramid Ski or snowshoe in on Livermore Road and ascend North Tripyramid via Scaur Ridge Trail. Traverse to Middle Tripyramid before returning the way you came.

Willey, Field and Tom From Crawford Notch, take the Avalon Trail over Mt. Avalon to Mt. Field and, optionally, continue to Willey or Mount Tom. Return on the A-Z Trail or Avalon Trail.

Mt. Clinton and Eisenhower Via Crawford Path, an opportunity to bag these two 4,000'-ers, with plenty of time above treeline. From Mt. Clinton to the Eisenhower summit is 1.6 miles.

Mt. Chocorua An 8-mile round trip via the Champney Falls Trail from the Kancamagus Highway. Finishes along the beautiful, exposed summit ridge. Crampons will usually be necessary.

For more winter hiking ideas, see *Snowshoe Hikes in the White Mountains* by Steven D. Smith or *Winter Trails: Vermont and New Hampshire* by Marty Basch.

The RMC's Log Cabin on Mount Adams   Ned Therrien

Mount Washington in Winter

The two recommended routes from Pinkham Notch for winter ascents of Mount Washington are **Boott Spur Trail** and a **variation on Lion Head Trail**. Either route involves an ascent of 4,100', with Lion Head (4.1 miles each way) taking about 8 hours for the round trip and Boott Spur (5.4 miles each way) about 10 hours. These estimates assume reasonable weather and trail conditions. Always check the status of your intended route at Pinkham Notch before setting out. The Lion Head winter route was relocated in 1996 due to avalanche problems. A winter ascent of Mount Washington is a serious undertaking and anyone attempting this must have full winter gear and adequate experience: Most serious accidents on the mountain occur in winter. The **Mount Washington Auto Road** provides another route to the summit although, at over seven miles, it is much longer than the two trails above. Note that in the winter, none of the summit facilities are open to the public.

20 | Backcountry Skiing

Tuckerman Ravine

This is the mecca for spring skiing in the Northeast! A dramatic glacial cirque high on the east side of Mount Washington, "Tuck's" is daunting terrain, with its 800' headwall attaining 50 to 55 degrees at the top. From late March into June the Headwall and nearby chutes attract thousands of skiers and spectators. Over the years nearly every gully and crevice has been skied, and thousands of New England skiers make the annual pilgrimage to Tuckerman Ravine for the spring skiing and fun in the sun.

The typical program is to hike up to Hermit Lake carrying your skis and, using one of the shelters as a base, spend a day or more skiing in the Ravine before skiing back down to Pinkham on the John Sherburne Ski Trail. Avalanches and falling ice in Tuckerman Ravine have claimed many lives over the years, so be sure to check weather and snow conditions in advance. The Forest Service carefully monitors the Ravine and posts daily bulletins for the main descent routes. Follow their recommendations!

Approach: *It is 2.4 miles from Pinkham Notch Visitor Center to Hermit Lake via the Tuckerman Ravine Trail. From Hermit Lake, climb the steep half mile to the base of the Headwall. The bottom of the Hillman Highway ski run is just a short distance from the Hermit Lake caretaker cabin.*

Left Gully *800-foot vertical; steepness: 40 degrees*
This is the large chute on the left side of the bowl. Left Gully is a favorite route—it is less intimidating than the Headwall or the Center Wall. There is usually a good ascent route on its right side, or up the Center Wall.

Center Wall *800-foot vertical; steepness: 50 degrees*
Perhaps the steepest sustained slope, the Center Wall's smooth flank maintains about 50 degrees. The Headwall is to the right of Center Wall. The most dangerous of the standard routes, the Center Wall's skiable lines vary depending on snow cover.

Tuckerman Ravine's Center Wall   Bob Grant

Headwall *800-foot vertical; steepness: 50-55 degrees*
Famous for its extreme pitch, the headwall gets the most attention
from skiers. Although it is much wider than the gullies and has a
good runout, it gets extremely steep towards the top, so be sure
you can handle the terrain before climbing too high.

Right Gully *800-foot vertical; steepness: 35-40 degrees*
This popular, relatively wide gully is located to the right of the
Headwall. It empties next to **Lunch Rocks**—the best place to
watch the action—near the base of the Headwall.

Hillman Highway *1500-foot vertical; steepness 35 degrees*
This popular and very accessible gully system on the north flank
of Boott Spur looms high over Hermit Lake. Two prominent gullies flow off the ridge and join, forming a great "Y". It is an unmis-
takable feature of the lower part of Tuckerman Ravine. Years ago
major alpine slalom races were held on Hillman Highway and in
Right Gully.

John Sherburne Ski Trail *2.3 miles*

This is the only ski route from the Ravine down to Pinkham Notch. It parallels Tuckerman Ravine Trail, and seven short connector links provide easy access between the two. Although steep in places (30 degrees), the Sherburne Trail is rated intermediate for alpine skiers. It is also popular with nordic skiers.

Descending from Hermit Lake: Hike down Tuckerman Ravine Trail or ski down the John Sherburne Ski Trail. Skiing down Tuckerman Ravine Trail is not permitted.

Forest Service Snow Ranger Brad Ray, on the job in Tuckerman Ravine
U.S. Forest Service

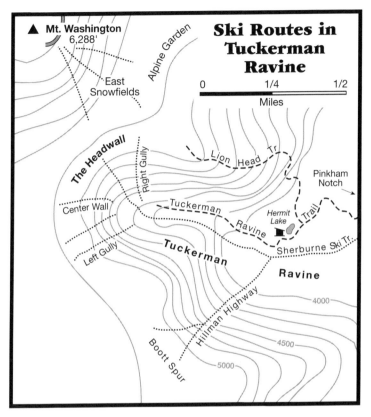

Ski Routes in Tuckerman Ravine

▲ Mt. Washington 6,288'

East Snowfields

Alpine Garden

0   1/4   1/2
Miles

The Headwall

Right Gully

Center Wall

Left Gully

Lion Head Tr.

Tuckerman Ravine

Hermit Lake

Pinkham Notch

Trail

Tuckerman

Sherburne Ski Tr.

Ravine

Hillman Highway

Boott Spur

4000

4500

5000

Skiing and Avalanche Safety Pointers

- Check avalanche bulletins and heed all warnings.
- When in doubt, double check or don't go. Never travel alone.
- If possible, avoid crossing steep, open areas of snow.
- Most avalanches occur during or immediately after snowstorms, but unstable slope conditions persist for days afterwards.
- Warming spring conditions dislodge dangerous blocks of ice.
- Bear in mind that snow conditions can change rapidly. Safe, mid-day corn snow will quickly freeze up in afternoon shade.

Other Alpine Skiing Near Pinkham

Gulf of Slides

Although much less visited than Tuckerman Ravine, the gullies and snowfields in the Gulf of Slides offer great skiing. For some, its size and openness bring western skiing to mind. This area does require a great degree of self-sufficiency and avalanche savvy: There are usually fewer people around, and rescues are more time consuming than in Tuckerman. Check the avalanche board at Pinkham to get a general idea of current avalanche conditions before setting out. A very enjoyable shorter trip is to ski up and down the 2.5-mile **Gulf of Slides Trail**, foregoing the steep stuff.

Approach: From near the south end of the parking lot at Pinkham Notch, follow signs for the Gulf of Slides Ski Trail.

Summit Snowfields

For skiers who want to get away from the crowds of Tuckerman, the wide open snowfields on Mount Washington's summit cone are a good alternative. The **East Snowfields**, located on the right above the Headwall, have a 30-degree pitch, which is much more forgiving than the alarming steepness of the Headwall or the Center Wall.

Approach: Via Lion Head Trail (use the winter hiking route), Right Gully or the Headwall.

Great Gulf

This remote (especially in winter) headwall is popular among some of the more hard-core skiers. Because it is north-facing, snow lingers in its gullies until late spring. It is really only advisable for experienced parties of very fit, expert skiers. Since skiing all the way down to Rt. 16 via Great Gulf Trail vastly diminishes the alpine flavor of the experience, climb up and out of the ravine when you are done for the day and return the way you came. Note that Great Gulf is a wilderness area; follow wilderness regulations.

Approach: Ascend Lion Head and traverse the Alpine Garden, or ski/hike up the Auto Road to the top of Great Gulf, a distance of seven miles.

Nordic Skiing at Pinkham Notch

Although the high-profile skiing is in the steep ravines, the lower wooded slopes offer excellent terrain of a more nordic character. Short trails in the immediate vicinity of Pinkham Notch lead to Wildcat Ski Area, Square Ledge, up to the Auto Road and down to Jackson village. These trails are not groomed, but a relatively new addition to the scene, **Great Glen Trails**, does provide a selection of tracked trails. It is located at the base of the Auto Road.

Avalanche Brook Trail is a fairly demanding nordic trail that contours south from Pinkham Notch for 5.5 miles to the Dana Place Inn on NH 16. Beginning as a mix of easy terrain with some climbing, it finishes with a steep descent to the highway. Here it meets the upper end of the groomed **Ellis River Trail** which provides a pleasant ski (4.7 miles) along the river down to Jackson village.

Wildcat Valley Trail is the area's classic backcountry, downmountain ski trip. From the top of **Wildcat Ski Area** (ride the gondola) drop down the backside for the 11-mile run to Jackson. Brief steep sections at the top are followed by moderate to easy terrain as the route ties into the Jackson ski trail network. A shorter version (8 miles) of this tour is possible by skiing down to the Dana Place on Rt. 16. Buy a trail pass in Jackson before starting out.

Connie's Way links Pinkham Notch with the Auto Road. Starting out on the **Old Jackson Road** (AT), it soon branches right and, holding a lower elevation, slabs across easy terrain, meeting the Auto Road one mile above NH 16. Thus it connects Pinkham Notch with the Great Glen Trails cross country ski area.

Hayes Copp X-C Trail meanders through eight miles of forest. It begins at **Dolly Copp Campground** (north of Pinkham) and ends at the boundary of the Great Gulf Wilderness. Difficulty ranges from easy to most difficult. There is currently no easy link (river crossing) between Hayes Copp and the Great Glen trail system.

Ski Tours in the Jackson Area

The 200-km network of cross country trails in and around Jackson village is probably the premier venue for tracked and light nordic skiing in the White Mountains. The **Jackson Ski Touring Foundation** runs the show from its full-service ski center in Jackson village. Information, ski rentals and maps of the trail network are available from the ski touring center. It is necessary to buy a trail pass if you plan to use any of the maintained trails.

Doublehead Cabin, on the top of North Doublehead Mountain, offers great views of the Presidential Range and Mount Washington. The cabin is only 1.8 miles from Dundee Road (upper Jackson) on the **Doublehead Ski Trail**. The usage fee is currently $20 per night, and there are bunks for eight. Contact the Forest Service (Conway office) for details.

From the end of Carter Notch Road (above Jackson), the **Wildcat River Trail** (first 0.7 mile is on **Bog Brook Trail**) runs over skiable terrain to **Carter Notch Hut**. A more challenging approach for skiers is the Nineteen Mile Brook Trail, the popular snowshoe route from NH 16. A visit to the hut (open year round) makes a good day trip. Contact the AMC for reservations for overnight stays. The hut is also the starting point for the climb of **Carter Dome** (4,832') and the circuit tour via Zeta Pass down to NH 16. This trip is recommended only for parties experienced in ski mountaineering.

Backcountry Skiing Adventures: Maine and New Hampshire, by David Goodman, is a good source for detailed information on the Carter Dome trip (above) and other White Mountain backcountry ski tours.

Ski Touring in the Zeeland Area

The Zeeland area offers some of the best backcountry *nordic* skiing in New Hampshire, with great wilderness trips of 10 or 20 miles (and more) possible. The AMC's **Zeeland Falls Hut** is open year-round and serves as a excellent base. In winter the hut, including the kitchen, is run on a self-serve basis, with caretakers in residence. Visitors must bring all supplies, including a warm sleeping bag. Call the AMC at Pinkham Notch (603-466-2727) for reservations. Most of the ski/snowshoe routes follow old railroad beds and thus are on very moderate grades. To reach the area, drive east 2.3 miles from the junction of US 302 and US 3 in Twin Mountain to **Zeeland Road**. The large winter parking area is just beyond, on the left.

Zeeland Road and Zeeland Trail

Beginning at Zeeland Campground on US 302, unplowed Zeeland Road climbs briefly before maintaining only a slight grade to its end at 3.7 miles. Continue on Zeeland Trail for 2.5 miles over rolling, gently climbing terrain to the **Twinway**. Zeeland Falls Hut is located a few minutes (right) up Twinway. For a pure ski trail approach to the hut, the 4-mile **Spruce Goose Ski Trail** provides a more challenging alternative to wide, monotonous Zeeland Road.

Thoreau Falls Loop (17 miles)

This is backcountry nordic skiing at its best. From Zeeland Falls Hut, ski south through dramatic **Zeeland Notch** on the **Ethan Pond Trail**, reaching **Shoal Pond Trail** after 2.6 miles. Pass Shoal Pond with its views of Carrigain and the Zeeland area and continue over easy terrain down to the **Wilderness Trail** at 6.6 miles (Stillwater Junction). Heading west (right), reach **Thoreau Falls Trail** at 9.2 miles. Turn north and pass **Thoreau Falls** at 14 miles. The trail is very steep by the falls. From here it is 2.5 miles back to Zeeland Falls Hut. Probably the majority of skiers simply ski out to **Shoal Pond** and back to the hut. This makes for an excellent moderate trip of 7 miles. Another easy-terrain option is to ski down to Stillwater Junction and back, a roundtrip of 13 miles.

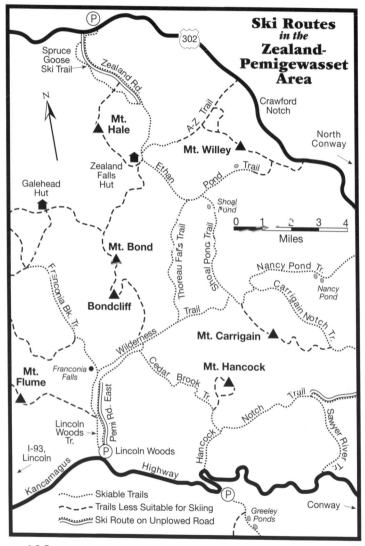

Ski Routes
in the
Zealand-Pemigewasset Area

302

N

Spruce Goose Ski Trail
Zealand Rd.

Crawford Notch

North Conway

Mt. Hale

A-Z Trail

Mt. Willey

Galehead Hut

Zealand Falls Hut

Ethan

Pond Trail

Shoal Pond

0   1   2   3   4
Miles

Mt. Bond

Franconia Bk. Tr.

Thoreau Falls Trail

Shoal Pond Trail

Nancy Pond Tr.

Nancy Pond

Bondcliff

Trail

Carrigain Notch Tr.

Mt. Carrigain

Wilderness

Mt. Flume

Franconia Falls

Cedar Brook Tr.

Mt. Hancock

Lincoln Woods Tr.

Pemi Rd. East

Hancock

Notch

Sawyer River Tr.

I-93, Lincoln

Lincoln Woods

Highway

Conway

Kancamagus

Greeley Ponds

·········· Skiable Trails
– – – Trails Less Suitable for Skiing
∼∼∼∼ Ski Route on Unplowed Road

198 • *Backcountry Skiing*

Kancamagus Highway

Scenic Kancamagus Highway provides access to excellent cross country skiing from a several trailheads. Views of waterfalls, high ridges, and ice-choked rivers await. Very accessible, with an extensive network of old railroad beds, the area is popular with beginners and long-distance skiers alike. It is really the complement to the Zealand approach, as Zealand gives access to the Pemigewasset Wilderness from the north, and the Kancamagus Highway provides access from the south.

Lincoln Woods Trail and the Wilderness Trail

Park at Lincoln Woods (5.5 miles east of I-93). From here the heavily used Lincoln Woods Trail, also called Wilderness Trail, begins with an impressive suspension bridge across the Pemigewasset River. Follow the old railroad bed (almost flat) along the river, arriving at Franconia Brook, and the wilderness boundary, after 2.9 miles. It's an ideal trail for pleasant, easy gliding. It is also the gateway to longer trips. After crossing Franconia Brook, the Wilderness Trail bears right and continues for another 6 miles, intersecting with other trails and providing access to Zealand Falls Hut, the Desolation area, and Hancock Notch. From Franconia Brook it is only a short half-mile jaunt up to the cascades of **Franconia Falls**.

Pemi East Side Road (3 miles each way)

Across the river from the Lincoln Woods Trail (above), the East Side Road runs over slightly hillier terrain. At its upper end are good views of Mount Bond and Franconia Ridge. A loop using Lincoln Woods Trail is possible, but only when snow conditions permit a safe crossing of the river.

Black Pond (3.4 miles each way)

After 2.6 miles on **Lincoln Woods Trail**, branch left on **Black Pond Trail** and climb up to Ice Pond. After skiing through the site of a former logging camp, reach Black Pond with its fine panorama of the surrounding mountains. Return by the same route.

Forest Service Ski Trails

Free info sheets, available from Forest Service Visitor Centers, describe the trails given below in more detail. None of these trails is groomed or patrolled: You are on your own.

The **Oliverian/Downes Brook Ski Trails** are 13 miles west of Conway, opposite the Passaconaway Campground. **East and West Loops** (2 and 1.2, miles respectively) are joined by a connector trail and offer a total of four miles of skiing. West Loop starts from the parking area for the Hedgehog Mountain and Downes Brook Trails, while East Loop begins at the Oliverian Brook Trail parking.

The **Upper and Lower Nanamocomuck Ski Trails** (9.6 and 6.9 miles, respectively) parallel the highway on the other side of beautiful, granite-choked Swift River. Both trails can be picked up from the parking area on **Bear Notch Road**, one mile north of the Kancamagus Highway. The lower trail, the easier of the two and suitable for novices, runs from Bear Notch Road past Rocky Gorge to historic **Albany Covered Bridge**. The interesting and more difficult upper trail runs west from Bear Notch Road, ending near **Lily Pond**, 18 miles from Conway. Note: The upper trail cannot be accessed (or exited!) except at its endpoints.

Nancy Pond (7 miles roundtrip)

The reward of a ski or a snowshoe into this area is access to three beautiful, isolated mountain ponds: Nancy, Little Norcross and Norcross. There are superb views once you reach the higher country, especially in winter, as the frozen ponds allow you to get out in the open more. From US 302, about 4.5 miles from Bartlett, take the **Nancy Pond Trail**. About 2.4 miles in from the road, at **Nancy Cascades**, the trail climbs very steeply. This will be quite difficult for most skiers, especially descending. But the skiing beyond the cascades to the ponds is enjoyable. From the ponds it is possible to continue to the **Wilderness Trail** which then provides you with a good skiable link on to the **Kancamagus Highway** or via **Shoal Pond Trail** to **Zealand Falls Hut**.

Telemarker blasts past a yurt in Phillips Brook   Heidi Wight

Phillips Brook Backcountry Recreation Area

The Phillips Brook area is a drainage basin north of NH Route 110 and a few miles east of the hamlet of Stark: Groveton and Lancaster lie farther to the west. Using a system of woods roads and trails, backcountry skiers have access to 24,000 acres of the northern forest and 200 miles of skiable trails. There are four gateway (auto accessible) yurts and seven high-mountain yurts, as well as a lodge on Phillips Pond which may be rented by individuals or groups. For reservations or information call (800) TRAILS-8 (872-4578), or check out their website at www.phillipsbrook.org.

With its relatively northerly location, the Phillips Brook area generally has excellent snow cover and a long season. The possibility of multi-day tours also exists—using snowmobile trails one can ski over to the Nash Stream drainage or north to Dixville Notch and beyond, to Pittsburg and the Connecticut Lakes.

Waterville Valley

Waterville Valley sits in a basin formed by the mountains enclosing the headwaters of the Mad River, including Sandwich Mountain, Mount Tecumseh, Mount Osceola, and Mount Tripyramid. The area has long been famous for its alpine skiing, but there is good groomed and backcountry skiing here as well. We present three of the more popular trips. See Chapter 14 for the Waterville Valley map.

Approach: Waterville Valley is located at the end of NH 49, 11 miles north of the Campton exit on I-93.

Greeley Ponds (6-7 miles round trip)

From the trailhead parking off Tripoli Road—or from the ski trail network—pick up the **Greeley Ponds Trail** about 0.3 mile in on **Livermore Road**. Basically an old roadbed, the trail offers little challenge but is a pleasant woods ski to wild, unspoiled **Mad River Notch**. Lower Greeley Pond is reached at about three miles. The ski route continues over easy terrain and down to the Kancamagus Highway, a total of five miles from Waterville Valley.

Livermore Road

This beautiful woods road makes for great skiing. From the hiker parking area just north of the resort complex, Livermore Road is well-marked and obvious. If you ski all the way to **Livermore Pass** you have covered about 5.5 miles. Turn around and ski back the same way. Livermore Road is the approach route for climbing North Tripyramid (4,180'), one of the classic and difficult hikes of New Hampshire.

Smarts Brook

On NH 49, about five miles before Waterville Valley, the Forest Service maintains a 6-mile network of cross country ski trails. They are intermediate to advanced and run over a variety of terrain. **Pine Flat Ski Trail** (0.7 mile) gives a good view of Smarts Brook Gorge.

Approach: From I-93, drive 5.5 miles up NH 49.

Mount Cardigan 3,121'

In the days before chairlifts whisked skiers up mountains, this area was a center for downhill adventure. With the rediscovery of non-lift, or backcountry skiing, the area is again drawing skiers. The mountain has a network of cross country and down-mountain ski trails on its east side, based around **Cardigan Lodge**, which is located west of Bristol. See Chapter 17 for directions to Cardigan Lodge and the trail map.

Alexandria Ski Trail

This trail is steep and exciting, yet wide enough to feel comfortable on. The maximum pitch is about 25 degrees. From the Lodge, follow the **Holt Trail** 0.8 mile and across a bridge to a three-way junction. The ski trail (0.6 mile long) continues straight ahead (the Holt Trail bears right at the junction) and climbs to the rocks just below the summit, where there are wide views to the north and east. With good snow, this a classic ski run.

Duke's Trail

A bit longer and easier than the Alexandria Trail, Duke's was cut about the same time, in the 1930s. It provides a mile-long run from its intersection with the Manning Trail high on **Firescrew** (Cardigan's north summit) down to Cardigan Lodge. Climb up behind Cardigan Lodge to pick up the bottom of Duke's Trail.

Mount Moosilauke 4,802'

Moosilauke has a long tradition of skiing and, after a period of declining activity, it is once again receiving a lot of attention from skiers. In particular, the Dartmouth Outing Club has been very active in recent years. Moosilauke's variety of trails and its large, open summit dome make it an exciting place to ski when conditions are right. The **Snapper** and **Gorge Brook Trails** are in good shape and are skied regularly, but they are relatively steep. A popular, more moderate trip (7 miles) is to follow **Hurricane Trail** to the **Carriage Road** and ascend it as far as the junction with the Snapper Trail. As an option—if conditions are good—you might

Near the summit of Mount Moosilauke   Robert Kozlow

want to continue up the Carriage Road: it is another 1.7 miles to the summit. In any event, ski down the way you came up. The **Carriage Road** is the most skiable route to the summit snowfields, as it is less steep than the hiking trails, although snowmobilers tend to maul it fairly thoroughly.

Another favorite trip—with a more nordic flavor—is the **Merrill Ski Loop**. From the parking area at Ravine Lodge, continue up the logging road, but bear right after 100 yards. Passing by **John Rand Cabin**, the trail makes a switchbacking climb and traverses Mt. Braley before joining the Ridge Trail. Head left and follow this back to the lodge area. A clearing on Braley provides a great view of Moosilauke.

The 1.5-mile access road to the Ravine Lodge area from NH 118 is not plowed, and it is an easy ski. The lodge belongs to Dartmouth College and is not open to the public. The base of the Carriage Road is reached via a 1.6-mile access road to Moosilauke Inn.

Franconia Notch State Park

There are two skiable trails through Franconia Notch. The **Pemi Path**, which was designed as a summer hiking trail, and the **Bike Path** (or Recreation Trail), a paved multi-use path which runs from the Flume parking area north past Cannon Mountain. The Bike Path offers better skiing (less snow cover needed and friendlier terrain), but it has the drawback of also being the snowmobile corridor through the notch. North of NH 18, and west of I-93, the old Route 3 roadbed provides good skiing (snowmobiles are not allowed) for two miles. It ends at NH 141. Thus a route of 6-7 miles is possible: from Flume parking, past Cannon Cliff and the Old Man of the Mountain, past Profile and Echo Lakes and north to NH 141, ending about four miles east of Franconia village.

Approach: The southern end of the bike path is at the Flume hiker parking area, on the east side of US 3.

Mount Monadnock State Park (Jaffrey)

A 14-mile network of trails runs along the bottom of the mountain, based out of the state parking lot. No hiking or pets are allowed on the ski trails, and there is a nominal fee on weekends; weekdays are free. The skiing is easy south of the parking lot. North of the lot an intermediate route to Gilson Pond offers good views of Pumpelly Ridge on Monadnock. Mount Monadnock State Park is located in Jaffrey; see Chapter 18 for driving directions.

Pawtuckaway State Park (Manchester)

Pawtuckaway is a heavily wooded area, with plenty of ponds and swamps. A rather poorly signed network of roads and trails runs throughout the park, thus the park map is very helpful. With adequate snow cover, the unplowed roads can provide good cross country skiing.

Note: Excellent free recreation maps of the state parks are available from Forest Service visitor centers and the Dept. of Parks.

Maps: Washburn: *Tuckerman Ravine;* Goodman; State Park maps.

Classic Hikes of the White Mountains

The 29 hikes noted below are, in our opinion, the outstanding hikes in the White Mountains. Most of them are fairly strenuous, and most involve ascents of 4,000' summits, but only about half of the 4,000'-ers make our list. On the other hand, the lower summits of Chocorua, Monadnock, the Moats, Cardigan, the Baldfaces, and the Mahoosucs do belong on a list of classic hikes. Page numbers refer to the full hike descriptions.

Tuckerman Ravine Trail on Mount Washington

It is 4 miles and over 4,000 vertical feet to the top of Mount Washington from Pinkham Notch. Past the Hermit Lake shelters, the trail climbs into the upper ravine and ascends the steep head-wall to the barren, windswept upper mountain.   *page 16*

Alpine Garden on Mount Washington

In May and June, the alpine flowers on the gentler slopes above precipitous Tuckerman and Huntington Ravines are in bloom. Approach via Tuckerman Ravine Trail, the Auto Road, or the Ammonoosuc Ravine Trail.   *page 22*

Mount Jefferson from Great Gulf

Hike up Great Gulf to the base of Jefferson. Ascend the extremely steep (ladders) Six Husbands Trail with spectacular views into Great Gulf. Return to Great Gulf via the Sphinx Trail.   *page 30*

Carter Dome and Zeta Pass

Start along Nineteen-Mile Brook, and climb to Zeta Pass. Head south along the spine of the Carter Range over Mount Hight and Carter Dome, descending into wild Carter Notch.   *page 33*

On the Six Husbands Trail, Mount Jefferson   Jared Gange

Mount Washington via Ammonoosuc Ravine

This is the most popular route from the west (Cog RR base). It is extremely steep in places, but has good hand and footholds, and reaches treeline just below Lakes of the Clouds Hut. Continue on Crawford Path (above treeline) to the summit.   *page 45*

Mount Eisenhower via Edmands Path

This carefully laid-out trail ascends the west side of Eisenhower with an even gradient. There are superb panoramic views from the open, grassy summit. Mount Washington looms impressively, only a few miles away.   *page 47*

Mount Jefferson's Ridge of Caps

Starting high, from 3,000-foot Jefferson Notch, the Ridge of Caps provides an exciting and direct route up Jefferson. The upper section is open and very exposed to weather. Steep at times, with scrambles up rock slabs.   *page 50*

Valley Way: Mount Adams and Mount Madison

Very popular route from Appalachia (US 2) to Madison Springs Hut at treeline. From the hut, climb Madison or Adams or both. Descend Valley Way, Airline, or Lowe's Path.   *page 52*

King Ravine on Mount Adams

A demanding route through awkward rocks and boulders in the recesses of a deep ravine. Ascend the headwall to reach the open, upper flanks of Adams, a short way below the summit. The return to Appalachia is via Airline or Valley Way .   *page 55*

Traverse of the Northern Presidentials

Can be done as a loop from Pinkham Notch, via the AT into Great Gulf and up to Madison Hut. Make the exposed traverse of Adams, Jefferson, and Washington, descending to Lakes of the Clouds Hut. Return to Pinkham via Tuckerman Ravine.   *pages 24, 60*

Mahoosuc Notch

This boulder-strewn passage is considered the most difficult mile on the Appalachian Trail. From Success Pond Rd., hike through Mahoosuc Notch to reach Speck Pond, Maine's highest.   *page 71*

Traverse of the Baldfaces

Climb through woods past Baldface Shelter onto Yosemite-like slabs of smooth granite to ascend South Baldface. Continue on a semi-open ridge for over a mile to North Baldface. Views of Tuckerman Ravine, Carter Range, and to the ocean.   *page 92*

The Moats

Hike in past the water-sculpted granite pools of Diana's Bath before ascending wide-open Red Ridge. Continue on the main ridge to North Moat, then descend steep ledges and slabs on the Moat Mountain Trail. Sweeping views from North Moat. *page 100*

Webster Cliff

An exciting clifftop walk with dramatic views into Crawford Notch. After climbing the steep south ridge of Mount Webster, continue along the ridge, with its many viewpoints, to Mount Jackson and Mizpah Springs Hut. *page 106*

Traverse of the Southern Presidentials

From Crawford Notch to Mount Washington, or the reverse, with numerous variations. Using Crawford Path to reach Mizpah Hut, continue over Eisenhower to Lakes of the Clouds Hut and Mt. Washington. Descend Tuckerman Ravine. *page 106*

Zealand Falls Hut to Galehead Hut

A classic 2–3 day trip. Hike into Zealand Falls Hut, continue past spectacular Zeacliff up across Mt. Guyot to South Twin's panoramic views, before dropping steeply down to Galehead Hut. Finish with the pleasant walk out to Gale River Road. *page 113*

Galehead Hut and South Twin

An easy beginning followed by a steep climb to Garfield Ridge. From the hut, climb directly to the high, open summit of South Twin. Sweeping views of the Pemigewasset Basin and from nearby Franconia Ridge to Carrigain and the Presidentials. *page 113*

Mount Carrigain's Signal Ridge

The 5-mile trek up high, isolated Carrigain traverses an exciting ridge before reaching the summit observation platform and one of the best summit views in the White Mountains. *page 115*

Franconia Ridge and Mount Lafayette

A long and at times steep climb up Falling Waters Trail brings you out onto spectacular Franconia Ridge, at about 5,000'. The traverse across Mt. Lincoln and Mt. Lafayette is probably the finest high ridge walk in the East. Descend Lafayette's steep, open slopes to Greenleaf Hut situated in exciting alpine terrain. *page 122*

The Kinsmans from Franconia Notch

A demanding 10-mile trip, offering superb views of Franconia Ridge, directly across the valley. Hike up past Lonesome Lake before continuing on steeper trails to the top. There is an optional short detour to beautiful Kinsman Pond.   *page 129*

Traverse of the Bonds

This remote, beautiful hike leads deep into the Pemi Wilderness. The 5-mile approach on old railroad beds is followed by a steep climb to Bondcliff's spectacular alpine perch. Slightly higher Bond and West Bond are a few miles farther on open ridges.   *page 134*

Mt. Osceola and Osceola East Peak

From Tripoli Road, it is pleasant, but solid 3.5-hike up Mount Osceola, Waterville Valley's highest. After taking in the view from the dramatic, clifftop summit, make the rugged, and in places extremely steep traverse over to relatively viewless East Peak, bagging another 4,000' summit.   *page 148*

Mount Chocorua via Piper Trail

Chocorua's pointed, rocky spire is a famous landmark and a popular subject for photographers. Just south of Conway, the Piper Trail provides a solid hike on a well-maintained trail to the top of this steep and interesting mountain. The bare rock summit area offers one of the very best panoramas.   *page 141*

Whiteface and Passaconaway

From Wonalancet, ascend Blueberry Ledge Trail over interesting mixed terrain, reaching a stunning viewpoint—the Lake Region lies to the south—just below the summit. Continue on Rollins Trail to Passaconaway, returning on Dicey's Mill Trail.   *page 144*

The Slides on North Tripyramid

Classic traverse of triple-summited Mt. Tripyramid. After an easy approach march on a woods road, ascend the very steep slabs of North Tripyramid, traverse the narrow, wooded ridge over Middle to South Tripyramid, and descend steep scree, returning to easy-going Livermore Road. *page 146*

Traverse of Welch and Dickey

Thanks to a fire years ago, this 4.5-mile, low elevation hike (only 2,600') offers more bare rock than most of the hikes in the state. About half of this moderate climb over two open summits is on exposed granite bedrock. Some fun scrambling here and there. Good views of Waterville Valley. *page 152*

Moosilauke's Beaver Brook Trail

From wild and beautiful Kinsman Notch, steep Beaver Brook Trail works its way up past a series of rushing cascades, often using iron rungs and stone steps. This is a long but rewarding route to Moosilauke's mighty summit and its far-reaching views. *page 160*

Mount Cardigan: Holt Trail and Firescrew

One of the toughest trails in the state, the Holt Trail ascends steep gullies and slabs on Cardigan's east face. Descend by crossing open terrain to the bare ledges of neighboring Firescrew, and down the Manning Trail to return to Cardigan Lodge. *page 170*

Mount Monadnock

It's difficult to identify one classic route up this most-climbed mountain in New England. Whether you use the standard White Cross–White Dot combination or the much longer Pumpelly Trail, the point is to reach the interesting upper mountain with its forested ledges which alternate with steep bare rock slabs before giving way to the pure rock of the summit. *page 180*

For the three mountains above—Monadnock, Cardigan and Moosilauke—it is the mountain itself that is classic rather than any particular route.

Official List of New Hampshire's 48 Summits Over Four-Thousand Feet

New Hampshire has, as do many other hiking and climbing areas around the world, an official list of mountains to climb. New Hampshire's summits over 4,000' are spread around the White Mountains, giving the hiker a good introduction to the region. Completion of the list is a significant achievement, whether you take one summer or many years. The AMC's Four Thousand Footer Committee recognizes individuals who complete this list. Other recognized lists are: the 100 highest summits in New England, the traditional Adirondack 46 summits over 4,000', and the 114 summits over 4,000' in the northeastern U.S. Perhaps the ultimate New England list is the list of 451 summits over 3,000'.

1. Washington	6,288'		25. Field	4,326'
2. Adams	5,774'		26. South Hancock	4,319'
3. Jefferson	5,712'		27. Clinton (Pierce)	4,310'
4. Monroe	5,384'		28. North Kinsman	4,293'
5. Madison	5,367'		29. Willey	4,285'
6. Lafayette	5,260'		30. Bondcliff	4,265'
7. Lincoln	5,089'		31. Zealand	4,260'
8. South Twin	4,902'		32. North Tripyramid	4,180'
9. Carter Dome	4,832'		33. Cabot	4,170'
10. Moosilauke	4,802'		34. Osceola East Peak	4,156'
11. North Twin	4,761'		35. Middle Tripyramid	4,140'
12. Eisenhower	4,760'		36. Cannon	4,100'
13. Bond	4,698'		37. Wildcat "D"	4,070'
14. Carrigain	4,680'		38. Hale	4,054'
15. Middle Carter	4,610'		39. Jackson	4,052'
16. West Bond	4,540'		40. Tom	4,051'
17. Garfield	4,500'		41. Moriah	4,049'
18. Liberty	4,459'		42. Passaconaway	4,043'
19. South Carter	4,430'		43. Owl's Head	4,025'
20. Wildcat	4,422'		44. Galehead	4,024'
21. Hancock	4,400'		45. Whiteface	4,020'
22. South Kinsman	4,358'		46. Waumbek	4,006'
23. Osceola	4,340'		47. Isolation	4,004'
24. Flume	4,328'		48. Tecumseh	4,003'

Hiking With Children

Although most of the hikes in this guide book are within the ability of motivated young hikers, our list here is based on shorter trips—generally four miles roundtrip or less. And we have chosen hikes with interesting attractions: a waterfall, a cabin, or a scramble up rock ledges. It is worth noting that trails that are difficult in the clambering and climbing sense may in fact be easier and more enjoyable for kids than for their parents. The page numbers correspond to the full hike descriptions.

Pinkham Notch-Mount Washington

Crystal Cascade
A beautiful cascading waterfall part way up Tuckerman Ravine Trail is the goal. The roundtrip takes about an hour. Energetic hikers may want to continue to Hermit Lake.   *page 40*

Hermit Lake
Climb Tuckerman Ravine Trail to the Hermit Lake shelters, where the deck beside the caretaker's hut makes a great lunch spot. The ramparts of Boott Spur and Lion Head tower overhead. The roundtrip is 4.8 miles.   *page 16*

Square Ledge
One of the better views in the White Mountains. The trail starts across the highway from Pinkham Notch Camp and climbs moderately, passing Hangover Rock along the way. The roundtrip takes about an hour and is 1.2 miles.   *page 42*

Alpine Garden
In late May and June the upper slopes of Mount Washington come alive with flowers. Access the Alpine Garden Trail from the Auto Road to enjoy this annual spectacle.   *page 22*

Gorham and Environs

Lookout Ledge

Lookout Ledge offers one of the best low-elevation viewpoints of the great, high mountain wall of the Northern Presidentials, Mount Adams in particular. There is a good view of the Carter Range as well. Round trip is 2 hours and 2.6 miles.   *page 64*

Pine Mountain

Mt. Madison looms over Pine Mountain; the result is a viewpoint that rivals nearby Lookout Ledge. The view east to the Carter Range is also good. Round trip is 2 hours, 3.5 miles.   *page 66*

Mascot Pond

Cross the Androscoggin River on a footbridge suspended from the railroad bridge and continue over moderate terrain (the beginning of the Mahoosuc Trail) to pretty Mascot Pond. Round trip is about 2 hours. A local favorite with families.   *page 66*

Evans Notch

Basin Rim Outlook

A popular trail, this hike climbs the western wall of the mountain enclosing Basin Pond. There's a great viewpoint from the rim down to the pond. About 3 hours round trip.   *page 93*

The Roost

This accessible top offers excellent views of the Wild River Valley, Evans Notch, the Carter Range, and Mt. Washington. Round trip is 1 hour, 1.8 miles.   *page 96*

Blueberry Mountain

A moderate hike to an open summit area. Blueberries in late July and August. Views to the Baldfaces and Evans Notch. Round trip is 2–3 hours, 3.8 miles.   *page 98*

North Conway and Jackson

Kearsarge North

Although a big hike for small kids—6 miles round trip and a climb of 2,600'—Kearsarge North is worth it. Mount Washington is only

Photo:
David Goodman

15 miles away, and many of the higher summits are visible. You will see the lakes in western Maine as well. *page 103*

Black Cap
As a shorter alternative to Kearsarge North, Black Cap, at 2,370', offers excellent views for much less effort. Both hikes start from Hurricane Road in Intervale. *page 103*

North and South Doublehead
These twin summits above Jackson village can be done by a couple of routes. Rent the log cabin on North Doublehead through the Forest Service. *page 103*

Diana's Baths

Diana's Bath is an exciting cascade, choked with large granite boulders. It is an easy 0.5-mile walk from the car.   *page 100*

Crawford Notch
Mount Willard

A short hike up gentle slopes to dramatic clifftop views of Crawford Notch's classic U-shaped glacial valley.   *page 110*

Middle Sugarloaf

Less than 3 miles round trip, Middle Sugarloaf is a natural goal for hikers camped at one of the Forest Service campgrounds on Zealand Road. Superb views of Mount Washington.   *page 112*

Arethusa Falls

A steep trail through beautiful birches leads to New Hampshire's highest waterfall/cascade, at 200 feet. An hour each way. *page 117*

Zealand Falls Hut

This neat little mountain hostel offers food and lodging during the hiking season. Just outside the door, a sparkling stream flows over smooth granite slabs.   *page 113*

Franconia Notch
Artist's Bluff

Popular with photographers, Artist's Bluff is the classic short hike in this area. It is a fun clamber up a steep, rocky trail to great views of Cannon Mountain and Franconia Notch.   *page 124*

Lonesome Lake

A moderate climb on an excellent trail leads to Lonesome Lake. Across the lake, the AMC's hut awaits. Get your feet wet on the soggy 0.8-mile loop trail around the lake.   *page 128*

Mount Pemigewasset

An 1.8-mile hike to a dramatic cliff edge. Excellent views, especially of nearby Franconia Ridge.   *page 130*

Kancamagus Highway

Greeley Ponds

Greeley Ponds, snuggled in dramatic Mad River Notch, shouldn't disappoint. Osceola's East Peak is high overhead. The Upper Pond is reached at 1.4 miles, the Lower Pond at 1.9 miles. *page 136*

Sabbaday Falls

Water chutes and basins scoured from granite are the main attraction here. This is a good short hike; the roundtrip will take about 30 minutes. *page 137*

Mount Potash

A 4.5-mile hike round trip, Potash offers great views for relatively little effort. The trail is across the highway from the Forest Service's Passaconaway Campground. *page 138*

Waterville Valley-Lake Winnipesaukee

Welch and Dickey Mountains

Great views and two miles of walking along exposed granite bedrock reward the hiker. Very steep in places. To complete the 4.5-mile loop, continue to Dickey and descend across low-angle slabs and along a clifftop. Round trip is 3–4 hours. *page 152*

The Rattlesnakes

The short climb up the Rattlesnakes is a local favorite. From the top of the Rattlesnakes, you look down on Squam Lake, 500' below, with its shimmering coves. The south-facing ledges offer plenty of places to sit and relax. *page 155*

Mount Major

A huge, open summit area with vast Lake Winnipesaukee spread out at your feet is your reward for this one and a half mile climb. Fun scrambling up the rocks below the summit. *page 158*

Central and Southern New Hampshire

Mount Cube

Mount Cube's rocky summit affords a good view of nearby Moosilauke. Although a fairly solid workout, Cube is a traditional hike for young hikers. *page 164*

Mount Cardigan

Cardigan is a beautiful mountain and a classic first hike. On the west Ridge Trail, mixed forest gives way to the bare ledges of the upper mountain. 2 hours, 3 miles round trip. *page 168*

Mount Kearsarge

In clear weather you can see Sunapee, Cardigan, Moosilauke, Franconia, Mount Washington, and many other mountains from this breathtaking spot. The better (and longer) hike is from the west, from Winslow State Park. About 2 miles round trip. *page 175*

Blue Job Mountain

A short, fun hike across granite ledges and around boulders to a fine, open summit. Views to Mount Washington, Boston, and the ocean. Located near Rochester. *page 176*

Pawtuckaway State Park: South Mountain

The short scramble over roots and rocks to the 60-foot lookout tower on the summit is the hike to do here. *page 177*

Mount Monadnock

The barren summit makes Monadnock feel like a much higher mountain. It is immensely popular with routes from all sides. A challenging hike for the youngest hikers, but most kids will be up to the trip. Plan on 3–5 hours, 4.2 miles roundtrip. *page 180*

Glossary of Mountain Terms

alpine   steep, mountainous terrain with narrow ridges and pointed summits. Characterized by a transition from temperate forests to the treeless, arctic zone.

arctic vegetation   plants found above treeline. Although they thrive in the harsh arctic environment, these plants are easily crushed by a hiker's boot, often taking years to recover.

blaze   paint marks on trees and rocks indicating the route. Typically 6" high and 2" wide. Major trails are usually white, side trails blue, but other colors are sometimes used.

cairn   stacked pile of rocks used to indicate a route. A series of cairns defines the trail across a treeless expanse.

cirque   a hollow scooped out of a mountainside by glacial erosion. Tuckerman Ravine is a cirque.

col   a high pass, or a shallow dip on a mountain ridge.

exposed   unprotected from wind and weather. And in the context of climbing, describes a spot with a severe dropoff.

frostbite   the freezing of skin, usually on the face, but in more serious cases, of the hands and feet.

glacial erratic   a boulder transported by a glacier from its original location. Erratics can weigh hundreds, even thousands of tons.

headwall   steep upper end of a valley or cirque.

hypothermia   lowering of the core body temperature. Marked by disorientation, uncontrolled shivering, and incoherent speech.

krummholz stunted, ground-hugging trees (spruce or fir) that live at treeline—the highest trees on the mountain.

ravine steep-sided gully or narrow valley on a mountainside.

scree see talus.

summit top of a mountain, especially for higher mountains.

switchback hairpin turns of a trail or road—the trail "switches back on itself."

talus a loose accumulation of rocks and boulders on a slope, usually at the base of a cliff.

tarn a small pond, located at a high elevation.

trailhead beginning of a trail, usually the lower end.

treeline elevation at which trees are less than 8 feet tall or become non-existent. Determined mainly by latitude and elevation. Usually a brief, well-defined transition.

tundra open areas in an arctic environment. In summer, usually grassy with bushes—gentle to moderate terrain.

waterbar rocks or logs placed at an angle across the trail to deflect surface water, thus reducing erosion damage.

whiteout dense fog—especially in the context of a treeless, snow-covered landscape.

windchill the cooling effect of wind, especially on exposed skin. The temperature is effectively lowered by wind, e.g. 30 degrees F and a 25-mph wind has the same cooling effect as 0 degrees F.

Recommended Books

Allen, Dan H. *Don't Die on the Mountain*. New London, NH: Diapensia Press, 1998.

Appalachian Mountain Club. *AMC White Mountain Guide*. Boston: AMC, 1998.

Basch, Marty. *Winter Trails: Vermont & New Hampshire*. 2nd Ed., Guilford, CT: Falcon, 2001.

Bolnick, Bruce and Doreen. *Waterfalls of the White Mountains*. Woodstock, VT: Backcountry Publications, 1993.

Gange, Jared. *100 Classic Hikes of the Northeast*. Burlington, VT: Huntington Graphics, 2002

Goodman, David. *Backcountry Skiing Adventures: Maine & New Hampshire*. AMC: Boston, 1998.

Howe, Nicholas. *Not Without Peril*. Boston: AMC, 1999.

Lewis, Cynthia C. and Thomas J. *Best Hikes with Children in Vermont, New Hampshire, and Maine*. 2nd ed. Seattle: The Mountaineers, 2000.

Randolph Mountain Club. *Randolph Paths*. Randolph, NH: RMC, 1998.

Smith, Steven D. & Mike Dickerman. *The 4,000-Footers of the White Mountains*. Littleton, NH: Bondcliff Books, 2001.

Smith, Steven D. *Ponds & Lakes of the White Mountains*. Woodstock, VT: Backcountry Publications, 1993.

Smith, Steven D. *Snowshoe Hikes in the White Mountains*. Littleton, NH: Bondcliff Books, 2000.

Waterman, Guy and Laura. *Backwoods Ethics*. Boston: AMC, 1993.

Waterman, Guy and Laura. *Forest and Crag: A History of Hiking, Trail Blazing and Adventure in the Northeast Mountains*. Boston: AMC, 1989.

Recommended Maps

AMC. *Mount Monadnock*. Boston: AMC, 1999
- - -. *Mount Cardigan*. Boston: AMC, 1998
- - -. *#1 Presidential Range*. Boston: AMC, 1998
- - -. *#2 Franconia-Pemigewasset*. Boston: AMC, 1998
- - -. *#3 Crawford Notch-Sandwich. Range* Boston: AMC, 1998
- - -. *#4 Moosilauke-Kinsman*. Boston: AMC, 1998
- - -. *#5 Carter Range-Evans Notch*. Boston: AMC, 1998
- - -. *#6 North Country-Mahoosuc Range*. Boston: AMC, 1998

The Balsams Wilderness Trail Map & Guide. Dixville Notch: The Balsams, 2001.

DeLorme Mapping. *Trail Map and Guide to the White Mountain National Forest*. Freeport, ME: DeLorme Mapping, 1998.

Map Adventures. *White Mountains Trail Map*. Stowe, VT: 2001.
- - -. *White Mountains Hiking*. 1998.

Randolph Mountain Club. *Randolph Valley and the Northern Peaks of the Mount Washington Range*. Randolph, NH: RMC, 1996.

State Park Maps: New Hampshire Division of Parks & Recreation, Concord.
   Franconia Notch, Mt. Monadnock, Pack Monadnock, Pawtuckaway, Sunapee

Topaz Maps. *New Hampshire Outdoor Recreation Map*. Watertown, MA: Topaz Maps, 1999.

United States Forest Service (USFS). Several maps, including: *Kancamagus Highway*. Acquire at Visitor Centers (Saco Ranger Sta., Info Ctr. at Lincoln, etc.)

Washburn, Bradford, surveyor. *Mount Washington and the Heart of the Presidential Range*. 3rd ed. 1:20 000 Boston: AMC, 1989.
- - -. *Pinkham Notch*. 1:5 000. Boston: AMC, 1995.
- - -. *Tuckerman Ravine*. 1:5 000 Boston: AMC, 1993.

Waterville Valley Athletic and Improvement Association. *Hiking Trails in the Waterville Valley Area*. Waterville Valley, NH: WVAIA, 1994.

Wilderness Map Co. *Crawford Notch*. 1:40,000. Twin Mountain, NH: Wilderness Map Company, 2002.
- - -. *Franconia Notch* 1:42 700, 1994.
- - -. *Kancamagus Highway* 1:42 700, 2001.
- - -. *Mount Washington* 1:26 000, 1995.
- - -. *White Mountains Hiking Guide* 1:62 500, 2002.

Wonalancet Out Door Club. *Trail Map and Guide to the Sandwich Range Wilderness*. Wonalancet, NH: WODC, 1995.

Topographic Map Sources

- AMC, Pinkham Notch, NH (800) 262-4455
- DeLorme Mapping, Freeport, ME (800) 227-1656
- Eastern Mountain Sports, Boston (617) 254-4250
- Eastern Mountain Sports, No. Conway (603) 356-5433
- I.M.E., No. Conway (603) 356-7013
- Map Link, Santa Barbara, CA (805) 965-4402
- Mountain Wanderer, Lincoln, NH (800) 745-2707
- U.S. Geological Survey (800) USA-MAPS

Organizations

Appalachian Mountain Club
    Club Headquarters, 5 Joy St., Boston MA   (617) 523-0636
    Pinkham Notch Visitor Center, Pinkham Notch, NH (603) 466-2725
    Hut Reservations and Workshops   (603) 466-2727

New Hampshire Division of Parks & Recreation   (603) 271-3556
    Dept. of Resources and Economic Development
    172 Pembroke Rd., Concord, NH 03302-1856
    Crawford Notch State Park   (603) 374-2272
    Franconia Notch State Park   (603) 823-5563
    Mt. Monadnock State Park   (603) 532-8862
    Mt. Washington State Park   (603) 466-3347

Randolph Mountain Club, Randolph, NH 03570

United States Forest Service - District Offices:
    Androscoggin Ranger Station   (603) 466-2713
      300 Glen Rd. on NH 16, just south of Gorham
    Evans Notch Ranger Station   (207) 824-2134
      18 Mayville Rd., Bethel, ME
    Ammonoosuc Ranger Station   (603) 869-2626
      Box 239 Trudeau Road, Bethlehem, NH
    Pemigewasset Ranger Station   (603) 536-1310
      127 Highland Street, Plymouth, NH
    Saco Ranger Station   (603) 447-5448
      33 Kancamagus Highway, Conway, NH
    Supervisor's Office / White Mtn. National Forest
      Federal Bldg. 719 N. Main Laconia, NH 03246   (603) 528-8721
    White Mountain Nat'l. For. Camping Reservations (800) 280-2267

Wonalancet Out Door Club, Wonalancet, NH 03897

Hiking Notes:

Index

Photo: Virginia Loughran

About the author:

Jared Gange has hiked and cross country skied in New Hampshire, Vermont and the Adirondacks for 15 years. He has hiked and climbed in the Cascades, the Rockies, the Alps, Norway, Pakistan, Nepal and Tibet. He has previously written a hiking guide for Vermont and one on the classic hikes of the Northeast.

The author wishes to thank Steve Smith, proprietor of the Mountain Wanderer Map & Book Store in Lincoln, NH, and the author of three White Mountain guides. He carefully reviewed the second edition manuscript, making many corrections and updates.

Forest Service personnel Rebecca Oreskes and Patti Dugan from the Androscoggin Ranger District were very helpful in preparing the first edition of this book. Anne Gwynne and Dick Bailey of the New Hampshire chapter of the AMC also provided very valuable comments and advice.

Other titles from Huntington Graphics

100 Classic Hikes of the Northeast
by Jared Gange

**Secrets of the Notch: A Climbing Guide to
Cannon Cliff and Franconia Notch**
by Jon Sykes

Hiker's Guide to the Mountains of Vermont
by Jared Gange

Wildflowers of Vermont
by Kate Carter

Make a Splash - Swimming Holes of Vermont
by Jason Minor

**An Ice Climber's Guide to
Northern New England**
by Rick Wilcox

Vermont Recreation Handbook
by Diane Carter, Kate Carter and Jared Gange

Huntington Graphics
P.O. Box 373
Burlington, Vermont 05402
(877) 652-9134
huntgraf@wcvt.com
www.letsclimb.com